Dream Home Mallo

WITH THIS GUIDE YOU ARE G
YOUR MALLORCA PROPERTY A   ⌄R
DREAM.

EDITION 1 / 01.12.2023 / VOLKER HUNZELDER

Volker Hunzelder

TABLE OF CONTENT

INTRODUCTION — 5

PURPOSE OF THE BOOK — 9

RESOURCES — 11

1. INTRODUCTION TO THE FASCINATION OF MALLORCA — 14

1.1. Why Mallorca? The Island's Allure — 14

1.2. Popularity and the Associated Prices — 22

1.3. The Development of the Real Estate Market — 23

1.4. Stability and Security of Investments in Mallorca — 27

1.5. Why is Mallorca so popular and why is Mallorca so expensive? — 28

2. ECONOMIC CONSIDERATION OF MALLORCA REAL ESTATE — 32

2.1. The current price trend and its reasons — 32

2.2. Predictions: Will properties in Mallorca become cheaper? — 34

2.3. Regional Price Differences: Where are Properties Most Affordable? — 41

2.4. Long-Term Perspectives: How Stable is the Investment? — 42

3. THE REGIONS OF MALLORCA AND THEIR DISTINCTIVE FEATURES — 46

3.1. Where to in Mallorca? A Guide for Beginners — 46

3.2. Top Regions and Their Advantages — 100

3.3. Hidden Treasures: Lesser-Known Regions	102
3.4: The Importance of Location and Its Impact on Price	104
3.5. Mallorca Real Estate, What to Consider?	105

4. PURCHASE PROCESS AND IMPORTANT ADVICE
110

4.1. Mallorca Real Estate: What to Consider When Buying?	110
4.2. The Safest and Fastest Method to Your Dream Property	112
4.3. Overview of Additional Purchase Costs	115
4.4. Annual Taxes and Fees for Property Owners	118

5. THE RIGHT PARTNER: REAL ESTATE AGENTS IN MALLORCA
120

5.1. The Importance of a Real Estate Agent in Purchasing	120
5.2. Selection Criteria: Which Real Estate Agent is Right for Me?	122
5.3. Recommendations and Pitfalls in Searching for a Real Estate Agent	124
5.4. Benefits of Professional Real Estate Services	126
5.5. How do I find my dream property most safely and quickly?	127
5.6. Which Real Estate Agent is Best for Me? Which real estate agent is right for me?	133

6. STRATEGY FOR BUYING REAL ESTATE
137

6.1. Preparation and Planning: The Key to Success	137
6.2. Market Analysis and Timing: When is the right time to buy?	143
6.3. Financing and Budgeting	145

6.4. Long-Term Considerations: Rental and Value Appreciation — 146

7. RESULTS AND VISION — 148

7.1. The Path to Property Ownership: An Experience Report — 148

7.2. The Goals of Property Purchases in Mallorca — 150

7.3. Long-term Perspectives and Value Development — 151

7.4. The End of the Journey: The Dream of Mallorca Realized — 153

CONCLUSION AND OUTLOOK — 155

SUMMARY — 157

NEXT STEPS — 158

ABOUT THE AUTHOR — 163

ACKNOWLEDGEMENTS — 165

COPYRIGHT © 2023 — 167

Introduction

Welcome, dear readers! You have just turned the first page of a book that has the potential to change your life in one of the most enchanting regions of Europe: Mallorca. This book is not just a compilation of facts, advice, and tips. It is a comprehensive guide that provides you with the tools to make your dream of living or investing on this sun-kissed island come true.

Why should you read this book in particular? There are, after all, many guides on real estate. The answer is simple: This book is specifically tailored to Mallorca. It considers the unique circumstances of the island, the local market structure, and the peculiarities of local laws and regulations. This makes it an indispensable compendium for anyone seriously considering putting down roots or investing here.

My name is Volker Hunzelder, and it was a personal concern of mine to compile this guide for you. It is based on my many years of professional experience in the Mallorca real estate market. Since 1998, I have been deeply involved with finding and mediating the perfect property for my clients on the most beautiful island in the world. I was fortunate enough to learn my craft at one of the most prestigious companies in the industry. Furthermore, I worked as the managing director of a luxury segment development company, allowing me to understand the real estate business on Mallorca from various perspectives. This guide is meant to help you guarantee that you find your dream property.

This guide aims to help you find your dream property safely and promptly. I want to show you a path that will assuredly lead you to your dream property with this manual. This path will protect you from the frustration of a fruitless search for your dream property and save you a lot of time.

The path to property acquisition is never easy, but it can be a journey that is much less stressful and more successful with the right planning and preparation. This is where this book comes in: It guides you step by step through every single aspect of the process – from creating a solid financial plan, to choosing your personal real estate expert in Mallorca, to successfully handling the purchase.

Within my 25-year career, there have been many changes in the entire search and purchasing process. Likewise, many details have been revised legally and fiscally. There have been many positive changes, but unfortunately also one or another negative change that has influenced buying behavior.

The internet did not exist in 1998, so I am familiar with the entire business from the analog era and learned the business back then. Of course, the internet is the main cause of these changes, both positive and negative. All information is available every day at any time, which makes your search, but also significantly simplifies the spread of offers. In this case, unfortunately, more information does not necessarily guarantee higher quality. Property buyers complain about how inaccurate the disseminated information on individual properties is. Moreover, the same property is often offered by different providers.

There are now approximately 1,000 official real estate agencies based in Mallorca. These 1,000 agencies employ about 6,000 staff members. The trend is rising. As a result, you are very confused and perceive the Mallorca real estate market as very cluttered and unprofessional. You need a lot of time to sort through the offers. Unfortunately, the multitude of offers does not guarantee the existence of these offers. One gets the feeling that the information was arbitrarily created. Then, when you find a property you like, you often must learn that it has already been sold or didn't exist at all. Spare yourself this chaos.

You may now be asking yourself, "Am I ready for this step?" Let me assure you: If you read this book to the end and follow the instructions it contains, you will not only be ready, but you will wonder why you didn't do it sooner. Each chapter is designed to take you a step further on your journey. And with the additional bonuses and resources that this book offers, you will gain an invaluable advantage over other buyers. Throughout this book, the most frequently asked questions will be answered and explained in detail. Why does the task present itself as difficult, or at least very different from the real estate market in your home country? I would like to achieve that you understand this different situation, to decide on the most promising process with this understanding. The focus of the entire process should always be the ownership and the associated enjoyment of your dream property.

Life is too short to just dream of living in one of Europe's last paradises. The time for action is now. The good news? You don't have to go this way alone. This book will be your faithful companion, a mentor that helps you make informed decisions and avoid pitfalls.

You are not just holding a book in your hands. You are holding a key to a new world full of opportunities, to a life you have always wanted. But a key is only useful if you use it. So, turn it, open the door, and step into your bright future under the sun of Mallorca.

The first step is always the hardest, but it is also the most important. Take it today. Take it now. And let this guide ease your journey.

To an inspiring and enlightening reading experience!

Warmest regards, Volker Hunzelder

Purpose of the Book

Dear Readers,

The aim of this book is clear and unmistakable: to empower you to make your dream of owning property on the beautiful island of Mallorca a reality. Whether you're looking to invest in a holiday residence, seeking a permanent home, or wanting to purchase an investment property – this book is your comprehensive guide.

You are not just holding a book, but a true treasure trove of information, advice, and strategies based on years of experience and expertise. But that's not all! We go beyond theory and offer you concrete, practical steps that you can implement immediately. This is a dynamic roadmap that will guide you from the initial idea to the handover of keys and beyond.
Why is this book so valuable to you? There are many guides that present real estate as a kind of "simple" investment opportunity. However, this book considers the uniqueness of Mallorca and provides you with local insights you won't find anywhere else. You will learn how to find the right partners, from real estate agents to legal advisors. You will discover how to assert yourself in a competitive market. And the best part? You will learn how to avoid all the potential pitfalls.

Don't just be a dreamer; become the captain of your destiny. There's a reason you're holding this book. Listen to that inner call and take control. Each chapter will bring you a step closer to your goal. Don't just read it—live it!

And remember: The journey of a thousand miles begins with a single step. Let this book be your first step. Take it boldly, take it wisely, but above all: take it now!

To new horizons, to your dream property in Mallorca!

Sincerely, Volker Hunzelder

Resources

You've made it this far! If you have worked through this book from beginning to end, you now possess a wealth of knowledge and are well-prepared to dive into the fascinating world of the real estate market in Mallorca. But your journey of learning does not end here. No, it is just beginning! The final chapter of this book is an invaluable reservoir of resources that will serve as your constant reference work.

In this section, you will find everything that can help you navigate the path to success. Each individual chapter has its value and should be carefully reviewed and, if possible, integrated into your planning. Why is this so important? Imagine you are a captain sailing through unknown waters. You need a good nautical chart, reliable instruments, and current weather data. The same applies to your journey through the real estate market. Every tool, every chapter, is another building block that helps you realize your dream project successfully.

The chapters listed in this book are designed to be relevant to every reader, regardless of your current level of knowledge. Are you a beginner? Here you will find foundational literature and simple calculators for initial estimates. Do you already have experience? Then look forward to in-depth analyses and insider information that will expand your expertise.

We have done everything to make this book as comprehensive as possible. However, the world of real estate is dynamic and always changing. That is why it is crucial that you remain active. Use the resources we provide, but also seek out new information yourself. Be curious, be hungry for knowledge, be insatiable in your pursuit of success!

Before you close this book and begin your journey, take a moment to reflect on all that you have already achieved. You are no longer the person who first picked up this book. You have grown, learned, and are ready to take your destiny into your own hands. You are ready, and the world is waiting for you. Let us take this amazing path together.

Inspired? Motivated? Then set forth, the future is yours!

Imagine having the chance to discuss all your burning questions, uncertainties, and specific challenges directly with an expert. A personal conversation where we analyze your individual situation together, develop a tailor-made strategy, and create a concrete action plan for your success.

Use the QR-Code and book your online Strategy meeting for free!

1. Introduction to the Fascination of Mallorca

1.1. Why Mallorca? The Island's Allure

Mallorca – the name alone sparks immediate enthusiasm in many people. But why is that? What makes this island in the Mediterranean such a unique and alluring place that it attracts millions of tourists and real estate investors year after year? In this subchapter, we aim to answer these questions and take you on a fascinating journey through the allure of Mallorca.

The first and perhaps most obvious attraction is the natural beauty of the island. Sand beaches that stretch as far as the eye can see, crystal-clear waters, and impressive mountain ranges provide a breathtaking backdrop for any kind of activity. Whether you like to relax on the beach, hike through the mountains, or simply enjoy the scenery – Mallorca has something for everyone.

Yet, the island offers more than just outward beauty. The culture of Mallorca is another magnetic factor that draws people from all around the world. From architecture and historical sites to a vibrant arts scene and culinary diversity – Mallorca is a melting pot of Spanish tradition and modern, international flair.

Already in the 1960s, Mallorca opted for tourism. Since then, it has been expanded and perfected. The focus here has been on tourism from English-speaking and German-speaking visitors. These two groups have always been the most loyal guests. German tourists have declared Mallorca their favorite island. Due to tourism, the largest tourist-utilized airport in the world was created, and Mallorca can be reached from the rest of Europe in approximately 2 hours by plane. Other regions in Europe have not developed this ambition, which is why Mallorca has become one of the hotspots and has been able to gain a significant lead. All this underscores the pronounced business acumen of the Mallorca population.

Now, you may be wondering, "All this sounds wonderful, but what does it have to do with real estate?"

The answer is simple: all these factors contribute to a strong and stable real estate market. People don't just want to visit the island; they want to live, work, and invest here. This makes the real estate market an exciting, yet complex arena that we will cover in detail in this book.

This fantastic accessibility has led many to desire acquiring their dream property here on their favorite island and to enjoy the Mediterranean lifestyle. The cosmopolitan nature and the friendliness of the Mallorcans, along with their warmth, continue to convince new admirers of the island, so that many people dream of fulfilling their own dream. Many people have already realized this dream by purchasing their dream property and enjoying the Mediterranean life to the fullest. Even though Mallorca has now reached a high-priced segment, there is a broad range of prices for many beautiful properties.

There are many reasons for this. For one, the climate invites people to visit the island throughout the year and to enjoy Mediterranean life. The assurance of being able to enjoy approximately 300 sunny days a year, while simultaneously appreciating the overwhelming natural beauty, combined with the friendliness of the people and the excellent infrastructure, is unparalleled.

Golfers, too, find their paradise in Mallorca. There are 23 official golf courses, of which 3 are private. Some of these are among the most beautiful golf courses in Spain and have already formed a huge fan base. With the right location of the dream property, you can often reach up to 15 golf courses within a 15-minute drive.

Additionally, the international flair is enjoyed here locally. The Mallorcans, as well as the residents and property owners, together savor this gem in the Mediterranean. There's a shared understanding because there's a shared love: Mallorca! Furthermore, the aspect of security is increasingly coming into focus. Compared to the mainland or major European cities, crime is very limited. Due to its island location, security aspects are easier to manage and control. Family is the highest value here, which is particularly well-guarded, and that's why many families have decided to move their primary residence to Mallorca.

Many businesspeople have moved their main residence to Mallorca, flying to the office with the first flight on Monday and returning to the island on Friday noon to enjoy the Mediterranean life and their family. Many celebrities have also discovered Mallorca for themselves and have taken up residence. Once the love for Mallorca is ignited, it doesn't let go. The entire infrastructure of Mallorca is aimed at being able to guarantee people a high quality of life in the long term.

The capital of the Balearic Islands, Palma de Mallorca, with its approximately 470,000 inhabitants, offers not only the largest yacht harbor in Europe but also the cultural center of the Balearic Islands. From Palma, all other areas can be reached within approximately 45 minutes by car.

The highly coveted southwest of the island can be reached in 15 to 30 minutes and offers international flair of the highest level. Here, the largest number of international guests has settled. The southwest has prepared itself through its excellent infrastructure for year-round use.

The west coast and the Tramuntana Mountains are under environmental protection and are part of the UNESCO World Heritage. Villages like Valldemossa, Deia, or Soller are bordered by high mountains and with their fabulous nature, nature lovers will find their delight.

The northwest, around the towns of Pollenca and Alcudia, also offers very high-quality real estate. However, here they have specialized in the summer.

Along the entire east coast with its picturesque bays, one can still find a very authentic Mallorca. The southeast, with towns from Santanyi to Llucmajor, is more oriented towards Palma and offers, besides the villages, a lot of open land for fincas. In the center of the island, one enjoys the Mallorca village life and the finca living.

And now the most exciting question: Could Mallorca be your next big investment? The chances are good! With its combination of natural beauty, cultural richness, and a stable economic environment, the island offers ideal conditions for profitable and secure investments in the real estate sector. Let yourself be seduced by the allure of Mallorca and discover the many opportunities that this unique place can offer you.

In the following chapters, we will delve deeper into the various aspects that make Mallorca one of the most sought-after real estate markets in the world. Stay tuned!

1.2. Popularity and the Associated Prices

The charm of Mallorca is irresistible, and that certainly comes at a price. Yes, the island enjoys a kind of cult status, but why is this reflected so clearly in the real estate market? In this subchapter, we will explore the mechanisms behind the popularity and associated prices that make buying property in Mallorca such an interesting, yet challenging, venture.

For one, the climate invites people to visit the island all year round to enjoy the Mediterranean lifestyle. The certainty of enjoying approximately 300 sunny days a year, combined with the opportunity to enjoy the overwhelming nature, along with the friendliness of the people and the excellent infrastructure, is unmatched.

Let's start with the obvious: the high demand for real estate on the island. Mallorca attracts an international audience – from tourists wanting to enjoy the sun-drenched beaches to businesspeople recognizing the strategic location and robust economy. This demand naturally drives up prices, as offerings are often scarce, especially in the most coveted locations.

But the high price is not just a result of demand; it is also a sign of quality. In many parts of Mallorca, properties represent exclusivity and luxury.

New buildings with modern design and top-class amenities, restored historic villas, apartments with sea views – each property seems to tell a story and make a promise for a high-quality life.

"But are these prices justified?", you might ask. The answer is often: Yes! Because behind the high costs there is often added value that comes in the form of location advantages, facilities, and ultimately, quality of life. And do not forget: A property in a sought-after location is also an excellent investment that is likely to appreciate.

What does this mean for you as a potential buyer? It means that you are investing not just in a piece of land or an apartment, but in a lifestyle, in a community, and in a promising financial future. In the coming chapters, we will look more closely at these aspects and provide you with practical advice on how to make the most of your real estate purchase in this paradise.

So, do not be deterred by the high prices; instead, see them as a sign of the incredible potential that Mallorca can offer you. The investment may be substantial, but the rewards could be enormous! Stay tuned and let's continue this exciting journey together!

1.3. The Development of the Real Estate Market

Welcome back to our fascinating journey through the real estate landscape of Mallorca! Now that you have a feel for the allure and the prices of the island, it's time to look at the bigger picture: How has the real estate market in Mallorca developed, and what does that mean for you?

Let's begin with some historical context. Mallorca was not always the luxury destination it is today. In the 60s and 70s, it was more of an insider tip for hippies and globetrotters. But then the tourism industry recognized the island's potential, and everything changed. Hotels sprang up like mushrooms, and the real estate market boomed. Over time, the offerings became more exclusive, and the image of the island transformed into what it is today: a luxurious paradise.

Golf enthusiasts find their paradise in Mallorca. There are 23 official golf courses, of which 3 are private. Some of them are among the most beautiful golf courses in Spain and have already built a huge following. With the right location of your dream property, you can often reach up to 15 golf courses within 15 minutes by car.

Water sports enthusiasts and yacht owners will find romantic spots along the entire coast of Mallorca to anchor or enjoy the Mediterranean lifestyle to the fullest in the authentic, as well as fashionable, yacht harbors. The beaches are in excellent condition. The yacht harbors, with their great berths, are second to none and offer very high-quality gastronomy and are magnets for many vacationers and yacht owners.

In addition, Mallorca is a hotspot for road cyclists. For many years now, Mallorca has been one of the most popular training destinations for professional international road cycling teams. Every year, many professional teams come to the island for training purposes in autumn, winter, and spring.

On our favorite island, you can find every type of road, allowing for all kinds of training sessions. In the south and east of the island, there are long flat stretches where you can train for tempo hardness, and there are also gentle but very steep sections for mountain tours where you can build strength for mountain climbs.

Meanwhile, thousands of amateur racers and recreational athletes come here to emulate the professionals and enjoy the spectacular nature of the island to the fullest.

But it's also a true paradise for hikers. Everywhere on the island, you can find breathtaking hiking trails. These have all been highly professionally described and are frequented by many hikers. One of the most spectacular areas for this is, of course, the Tramuntana Mountains, which stretch across the entire west side of the island from the south to the north.

Here you walk through the UNESCO World Heritage site of such breathtaking beauty that it takes your breath away. You can find refreshment in many mountain inns and villages where you can experience the typical Mallorca life. But also, in other areas of Mallorca, you can explore the island on a high number of tours by hiking.

The entire infrastructure of Mallorca has been aimed at ensuring a high quality of life for people in the long term. The capital of the Balearic Islands, Palma de Mallorca with its approximately 470,000 inhabitants, not only offers the largest yacht harbor in Europe but also the cultural center of the Balearic Islands.

But that's not all. Mallorca also has a lesser-known side as a sustainable and ecological haven, where many environmentally conscious developers and homeowners focus on sustainability and preserving the island's natural beauty. Such projects add another dimension of attractiveness and attract a new kind of investor.

What does this development mean for you? It indicates that the market is multi-layered and dynamic. Here you will find offers ranging from historic fincas to ultra-modern luxury villas. This mix makes the market both exciting and complex, and that's exactly what you should see as your opportunity. The diverse market offers opportunities for every taste and budget. Whether you are looking for a return on investment, a dream residence, or both – Mallorca has the answer.

View this development as your springboard. It is your chance to move in a market that is not only rich in opportunities but also rich in history and culture. Your dream home may already be waiting for you; it could be a restored finca in the countryside or a chic apartment in Palma. The choice is yours!

Before we dive into the next chapters, take a moment to think about your own goals and ideas. How does your dream fit into the dynamic history of Mallorca? Prepare yourself to answer these questions in the following chapters. The journey of your life has just begun!

1.4. Stability and Security of Investments in Mallorca

One of the crucial factors in any investment, especially in real estate, is of course the stability and security of the market. If you are interested in Mallorca, you can take a breath: You have chosen one of the safest and most stable real estate markets in Europe.

Why is that? Mallorca is not only a popular holiday destination but also a living space that benefits from a stable economy and a high quality of life. The warm climate, breathtaking landscapes, and rich culture attract a wide range of people year after year: from tourists to businesspeople, from young families to retirees. This diversity ensures a constant demand for property and keeps prices stable.

But it gets even better! Mallorca has proven in recent years that it can withstand economic turmoil. Even during the economic crisis that shook many countries, property prices in Mallorca remained relatively stable. This is a sign of a robust market that offers opportunities even in difficult times.

There is also a wide range of property types and prices, which allows for different investment strategies. From luxurious seaside villas to charming townhouses in Palma, the possibilities are endless. And the best part is that quality is a priority here. This means that even if you invest in a less expensive property, you can be sure that you are making a solid investment.

What does this mean for you? It means that your investment in a Mallorca property is not just a step into a new life full of sun and culture but also a wise financial decision. You can buy your dream property with the confidence that your investment is protected and will appreciate over time.

You have already taken the first step into a bright future by picking up this book. It is now time to open the door to a world full of possibilities, stability, and security. Take the next step, and you will soon realize that your dream of a property in Mallorca is more than achievable. It is your chance to invest in a more stable, safer, and brighter future!

1.5. Why is Mallorca so popular and why is Mallorca so expensive?

The fantastic accessibility makes it very easy for tourists and property owners to reach our favorite island as quickly as possible.

The consequent increase in quality of life is priceless, and one enjoys to the fullest the Mediterranean lifestyle. This fact is greatly appreciated by people.

The reason for the high property prices lies in various circumstances. Tourism guarantees the accessibility of the island, and 300 sunny days contribute to this. The mild winter additionally invites you to escape the bad weather.

However, space on the island is limited. Classic land expected for future development, as we know from the vicinity of metropolises, does not exist on the island. All existing building plots are fixed in the general development plan. These plots will be developed in time.

It's important to know that approximately 90% of Mallorca consists of nature reserves and farmland, and thus is not buildable. Only about 10% of the land is designated as building land. This means that Mallorca has now reached a phase where there is little free building land available.

This free building land is in the outskirts of our capital city, as well as in the already built-up urbanizations. Nevertheless, this free building land most often does not belong to the Prime locations were naturally the first to be developed. Therefore, if a prime location does appear on the market, it commands top prices. The majority of the remaining free building plots are so-called remnants, which have not found a buyer yet due to their location and characteristics.

The construction industry has had to adapt and is now heavily involved in renovation and restoration work. Likewise, older properties are being replaced by new ones. The quality of construction has improved manifold in recent decades, so that the highest standards of quality are being met. The high quality of craftsmanship and especially the selection of premium materials have raised the standard to a new level, and Mallorca has become a trendsetter in this regard throughout Europe.

The high demand continues unabated with a limited supply. The German-speaking prospective buyer is still among the most financially potent. However, he is not the only interested party. Due to Brexit, we are currently seeing a slight decline in British prospects. In my estimation, however, this is only a minor dent, which will relax over time. For several years now, Scandinavian buyers have also discovered their love for Mallorca. Our Scandinavian guests are establishing themselves as the next very strong group of buyers. In the future, some new real estate interested parties from the United States and Canada will also be added.

Three years ago, Mallorca opened the first direct flights between the United States and Mallorca, greatly simplifying accessibility for U.S. and Canadian citizens to reach the island directly. For some time now, we have also been receiving interesting inquiries from the United States and Canada. A large fan base for Mallorca is also developing there. Owning a property in Europe, and additionally a property on the most beautiful island in the world, is very attractive for Americans and Canadians.

Very high annual price increases continue to be recorded. Investing in your dream property is always a good decision, as it is probably one of the few investments you can physically enjoy at the same time.

Often, properties are only held for 3 to 5 years before being resold. This is because the family's needs have changed over this time. Due to the usual annual rate of price increase, not only is the investment secured, but one sells the property at a profit to a new happy owner. The decision to acquire a new property is thereby simplified.

2. Economic Consideration of Mallorca Real Estate

2.1. The current price trend and its reasons

So, you have taken an interest in the enchanting island of Mallorca, and who could blame you? But before you dive fully into your real estate adventure, it is crucial to understand the economic context, especially the current price trends. Worry not, we will not leave you alone in this!

The prices for real estate in Mallorca have been steadily rising in recent years, but why is this the case? A primary reason is the island's unbroken appeal. Mallorca offers a year-round mild climate, beautiful beaches, and a thriving cultural scene. This makes the island attractive not just for tourists, but also for permanent settlers from all over Europe.

Tourism itself is, of course, a significant price factor. It creates a high demand for rental properties, especially in the sought-after coastal areas. This constant demand keeps returns high, thereby contributing to an increase in property prices.

But there are also domestic economic factors at play. The local economy is strong and diverse, with a focus not only on tourism but also on trade, craftsmanship, and technology. This varied economic structure makes the island less susceptible to economic fluctuations and contributes to the stability of property prices.

Over the past few decades, the Mallorca real estate market has developed into a significant entity in Europe. Continuous price increases have therefore become the norm. Even during the financial crisis around 2008, prices were very stable. The international clientele, from the seller's side, did not reduce prices, as the properties for sale were held by this international clientele. After all, these properties continued to be used by the families as their vacation homes.

And let's not forget the high quality of life. The excellent schools, healthcare facilities, and public services make Mallorca an ideal place for families and the elderly, which also contributes to price stability.

What does all this mean for you? It means that an investment in Mallorca real estate not only provides a fantastic way of life but is also a sound economic decision. You are investing in a market with substantiated, understandable reasons for its growth and stability.

That's great news for anyone considering entering the Mallorca real estate market. You are on the threshold of one of the most exciting and profitable phases of your life. Do not hesitate, take the next step! Your dream home on this sunny island is not just a luxury but also a wise investment in your future. Walk this path with confidence!

2.2. Predictions: Will properties in Mallorca become cheaper?

Now you are up to date with the current price trend in Mallorca, but you must be wondering: What does the future hold? Will properties on this paradisiacal island become cheaper, or will the market remain as robust as it is? It's good that you're here because we're about to clear up this very question!

First, you should know that property investments always require a long-term strategy. Speculations about short-term price drops can be risky. But don't be discouraged; the bigger picture is quite promising!

Since 1998, I have been involved in the Mallorca real estate market. Many years as a freelance worker for renowned brokerage firms and as the managing director of a property development company. Over the years, many of my clients predicted that property prices in Mallorca would fall. They were all proven wrong. Even today, this assumption persists among some clients. Many my current regular clients regret not having invested more several years ago. Due to high demand and limited space on Mallorca and the other Balearic Islands, high price increases continue to be recorded.

Current forecasts indicate that property prices in Mallorca will remain stable or even continue to rise. The main reason for this is the steadily growing demand from both domestic buyers and international investors. The island continues to attract people from all over the world, and if this remains the case, it is unlikely that prices will dramatically fall. Another factor is the limited availability of land. Mallorca is an island, which means that space for new developments is limited. This increases the exclusivity of existing properties and makes them an even more attractive investment.

As an example, I always like to refer to building land in a prime location in Nova Santa Ponsa. The local mountain in Santa Ponsa is affectionately called the Ensaimada. This name comes from the arrangement of the street layout and finds its comparison in the Majorcan pastry because this pastry is laid out in a snail shape. In the mid-1980s, you could buy a building plot in a prime location on this said Ensaimada for about 10€ per square meter. Today, depending on the location, the price per square meter of the building plot is about 2500€, with an upward trend.

Several billion euros have already been invested in Mallorca. In the coming years, international investors from all over Central and Northern Europe as well as from the United States and Canada will continue to invest on the island. However, as space on our island is not multiplicable, I look to the future positively. The urbanizations and localities of the island are already about 95% complete. Therefore, undeveloped building land is rare. As already mentioned, there is no expectation land for future development.

In all the publications I am aware of, the average square meter prices are always mentioned. This is certainly correct and understandable to get a rough overview. However, you should know that all properties obviously have an influence on this. The international clientele is primarily interested in the best locations and qualities. They do not want to invest in the city's belt of affluence, in social hotspots, or in very simply equipped properties and live their dream.

From my experience, it is very important for international clientele to fully enjoy their stay, which in turn leads them to look around in very good locations. In these locations, the rates of price increases are above average. On an annual average, the rate of price increase is about 5 to 7%. However, in top locations in recent years, price increases of 15% have also been achieved. Occasionally even up to 25%.

These properties are subject to different laws of market behavior. Units with beautiful sea views achieve the highest price increases here. There is even a price gradient between properties on the first sea line and those that also have a beautiful sea view but are set back further.

On the other hand, there is also a very large fan base for high-quality village houses and luxury fincas. Here too, top prices are achieved. Mallorca's real estate market offers the right property for all interested parties.

Each client pursues a dream of how they want to spend their time. These dreams are very different. One client wants to enjoy the beach life and is willing to accept higher humidity. Another client wants to enjoy nature and tranquility on their finca. Needs and tastes vary greatly.

As you have already learned, a price increase for properties in Mallorca is unstoppable. I have been dealing with the Mallorca real estate market for over 25 years now. Over the years, one or another client believes that price reductions will occur, which has never happened.

In fact, demand is consistently at a very high level. In connection with the details already mentioned, there is no reason to assume that price concessions will be made or that prices will stagnate. On the contrary. Prices will continue to rise steadily.

Mallorca has been part of the high-priced segment for many years. So-called bargains are no longer to be found in Mallorca. However, your personal real estate expert in Mallorca guarantees you a purchase at a serious market value.

Therefore, it is not only a very right decision to invest in Mallorca. It is also a very good decision because the investment made is a secure investment. If you decide on a good property in a high-quality location, you can only win.

Another important point I would like to revisit is the limited space amid consistently high demand. This circumstance is additionally caused by the absence of so-called expectation lands for building. The island's general building plan already identifies all possible building lands.

Of course, the designated building lands will be built upon. However, there is also the guarantee that at the edge of municipalities or cities, there will be no possibility to turn formerly agricultural land or green zones into building land. Expectation lands for future development, therefore, do not exist. This is also a very important aspect for the stability of prices and the positive future price development.

Mallorca consists of approximately 90% agricultural land or nature reserves. The existing building land is already about 95% built up, so we are now at the end of the development. The consistent demand with the tendency of ever-increasing demand from clients from all over the world is one of the most important facts that will trigger further steady price increases. Mallorca is still booming and continuously attracts thousands of new fans. A great deal of wealth will additionally be released in the coming years through the next generations of heirs.

According to a very successful Luxembourg wealth manager, this capital is of an unprecedented scope. This generation of heirs will most likely traditionally invest a part of their inheritance in Mallorca as well. After all, Mallorca is one of the safest investment places in Europe. Many new prospects will be gained who want to fulfill their dream. This continuous flow of existing and new customers will remain.

It is also remarkable and interesting that the existing property owner remains a customer. Even after the sale of his property, he remains loyal to Mallorca and looks for a new property. This means that this customer does not leave Mallorca but is searching for a new dream property.

The expansion and improvement of tourism and the associated perfect accessibility, while simultaneously increasing the quality of life, will unfortunately not make Mallorca cheaper. For these reasons, I continue to recommend investing. The prices in Mallorca will continue to develop positively. There are no signs of price reductions.

In addition to all the previous explanations, the psychology of this process must also be considered. Decades ago, these desires were awakened when the first property buyers from abroad discovered Mallorca. Since then, this process has continued to evolve.

Probably relatives or friends have already fulfilled their dream as well. As a result, social networks have been created, which additionally motivate new prospects to fulfill this dream. One does not easily let go of such a dream. This fact also contributes greatly to the fact that the demand is steadily present and continues to rise.

Of course, there are also economic uncertainties such as geopolitical tensions or global financial crises that could influence the market. But even in such scenarios, properties in Mallorca have shown amazing resilience in the past. They are considered "safe havens" in turbulent times.

So, what does this mean for you? It means that your timing could be perfect! You are facing the opportunity to enter a valuable, stable, and attractive market. If you act now, you could significantly benefit from future price increases.

Understandably, many prospects wish for prices in Mallorca to drop, or at least to stabilize. Since I have been active in the Mallorca real estate market since 1998, a continuous price decrease has been predicted to me. However, this decrease has never materialized, so we should now assume that prices will continue to develop positively, and we should learn from history. Even if it sounds incredible or even arrogant to most prospects.

Please assume that it will be more advantageous for you to find your dream property promptly. You should be mindful to find your independent real estate expert as quickly as possible, who will successfully complete the search for your dream property individually for you. This will enable you not only to enjoy your dream promptly but also to be able to buy more cheaply today than soon.

The outlook is clear: properties in Mallorca offer a fantastic opportunity for savvy investors like you. This is more than just buying a house; it is a leap into a bright, profitable future. Dare to take the next step. Your dream of a property under the sun is within reach and financially smart. Don't miss this opportunity!

2.3. Regional Price Differences: Where are Properties Most Affordable?

Imagine sitting in your future home in Mallorca, enjoying a breathtaking view of the sea, and thinking about how wise your investment was. Does it sound like a dream? Not necessarily. You just need to know where to look!

Mallorca is an island of contrasts, and this is also reflected in the property prices. While places like Palma or Puerto de Andratx are considered luxury destinations with correspondingly high prices, there are still regions on the island that are true gems for cost-conscious buyers. So, if you're looking for a more affordable entry into the Mallorca real estate market, consider areas like Llucmajor or Felanitx. These areas offer not only wonderful landscapes and good quality of life but are also significantly more affordable than the island's "hotspots." But don't wait too long! The lesser-known areas are becoming increasingly popular as more people discover the diversity of Mallorca. And as demand rises, so will prices.

You may now be wondering how to make the right decision with so many options available. Don't worry, the solution is simpler than you think! Create a list of your priorities: What is most important to you in a property? Is it proximity to the beach, local infrastructure, or perhaps peace and seclusion?

With a clear idea of your desires and needs, you can specifically search for regions that best fit your budget and life goals. Combine your dreams with smart planning, and you will soon find a piece of paradise that perfectly suits you.

Think of it as a treasure hunt where the treasure is your future home. And believe us, this treasure is worth every penny! Don't miss this opportunity and take the first step towards your dream life in Mallorca. Your future self will thank you.

2.4. Long-Term Perspectives: How Stable is the Investment?

Have you ever considered that your decision to invest in property in Mallorca could be much more than just a short-term adventure? Good, because you're on the right track! We will show you why an investment in Mallorca's real estate market is not only exciting but also stable and rewarding.

Over the years, the island has established itself as a true magnet for tourists and real estate investors alike. And there are good reasons for this. The robust economy, thriving tourism, and high quality of life make Mallorca a haven for your capital.

Just through the rates of price increase alone, one can already achieve a profit from a resale after 3 to 5 years, or at the very least, get the entire investment back and have enjoyed this investment to the fullest in the meantime. Should one then update their property to the latest standards and carry out high-quality renovations, the profit can multiply.

In retrospect, one can see that Mallorca has emerged not only unscathed through all crises over the last 40 years but as a big winner. Of course, it's not only due to the high-quality and stunningly beautiful properties that Mallorca has maintained its position but also because of the continuously improved infrastructure and the very wise economic policy of the Balearic Islands.

As an autonomous region of Spain, the Balearics have what is known as an island council. Consequently, the central government in Madrid does not exclusively determine what is implemented in Mallorca. Even if it sometimes seems a bit cumbersome, one must credit the island council with having protected the islands from overdevelopment. Unlike other regions of Spain, like the mainland, where the mistake of focusing only on mass was made, care was taken to ensure that the islands can continue to showcase their spectacular nature and not lose their appeal.

The locals, the Mallorquins themselves, as well as the residents, want to preserve the Balearics as they are. On the other hand, tourism and the entire real estate sector are the most important sources of income. For this reason, care is taken to ensure that the infrastructure is continuously improved.

Mallorca aims to remain a destination for mass tourism on the one hand, while on the other hand, the quality of tourism is to be raised. There has been a lot of sensitivity in working on this for years, and it will continue to occupy us for the coming years.

It is a Herculean task that cannot be implemented ad hoc, as processes have been established over decades of tourism that cannot be abolished overnight. It is about adjusting certain screws. Everyone is aware that mass tourism is the main source of income for Mallorca and its inhabitants.

With the change in local politics in 2023, there is now also a strong emphasis on promoting social housing construction. Unfortunately, this process has been very much neglected in many previous years, so there is a great need to catch up in this segment. This will generate positive effects.

On the one hand, this naturally promotes social peace on our favorite island and ensures that people with lower incomes can live in an adequate property. On the other hand, it will trigger positive effects among investors and make the location Mallorca appear even more attractive. The San Joan de Palma de Mallorca airport is currently reaching a new level through renovation works, preparing it to remain competitive for the coming years. Accessibility will also be guaranteed in the coming years.

But it's not just about the present. Looking to the future: The continuous development of infrastructure projects, the pursuit of sustainability, and the increasing attractiveness as a place of residence for digital nomads and expats ensure a sustainable increase in the value of your property. Your decision today may prove to be one of the best of your life. Do you believe in the power of diversification? Your opportunity lies in Mallorca as well. The island's real estate market offers a wide range of investment possibilities, from luxury villas to charming fincas. Each asset class has its own advantages and risk profiles, allowing you to find the ideal balance for your portfolio.

You might now be asking yourself, "But what if times get tough?" Of course, there is no guarantee without risk, but Mallorca's geographic and cultural diversity acts as a natural safety net against economic fluctuations. This makes your investment much more stable than you may think. You see, investing in real estate in Mallorca is much more than just a purchase; it's an entry into a world of opportunities, stability, and potential prosperity. So, what are you waiting for? Take the initiative, and your future self will thank you, living in a dream home under the Mallorca sun. Do it now!

3. The Regions of Mallorca and Their Distinctive Features

3.1. Where to in Mallorca? A Guide for Beginners

Welcome to one of the most exciting chapters of your property journey! You're faced with one of the loveliest decisions of your life: Where on the idyllic island of Mallorca would you like to settle? The answer is not as straightforward as one might think, for Mallorca is an island of contrasts, with something to suit every taste.

It is indeed a very difficult question because it individually concerns your quality of life. The entire island of Mallorca has magical attractions everywhere. As the saying goes: one person wants to live so close to the water they can spit cherry pits into the sea. Other dreams of lying in a hammock strung between the palms on their finca, enjoying the peace and nature. Tastes and preferences vary that much.

As you already know from me, I can find something to appreciate in all of it. Now, however, it comes down to you personally and your personal lifestyle. The infrastructure across all of Mallorca has been developed to such a high standard that one can reach various points on the island within 30 to 45 minutes. So, if you dream of a finca in the middle of the island, you can expect to quickly reach one of the coastal sections. Likewise, you know that a car is indispensable to cover these distances.

Someone who wants to feel the international ambiance around them should carefully consider whether a finca is right for them. For these customers, the city of Palma and, of course, the entire southwest of the island stand out as hotspots.

Similarly, there will be customers who simply want to reach the airport very quickly and are not looking for denser settlement. For this purpose, the southeast naturally presents itself.

"After all the years I've lived on Mallorca, this island has become my home. I'm still German in my head, but Mallorquin at heart. It's all been worth it!"

More and more customers, however, want to escape the hustle and bustle and are looking around in other regions of Mallorca. The east coast captivates with its small bathing coves and the more tranquil and authentic Mallorca.

Even the north up to the northwest has beautiful small villages and small bathing coves combined with long white beaches. The Tramuntana Mountains stretch along the entire west coast and are part of the UNESCO World Heritage. The nature here is breathtaking and invites for long hikes. Here one can find many olive groves and citrus plantations nestled among pine forests that provide plenty of shade for hikers.

In the villages, one can enjoy the typical Mallorca village life and let one's soul dangle. Here too, my recommendation is to seek intensive advice to find the optimal spot for oneself. The internet also offers a multitude of possibilities to obtain meaningful information in advance.

Imagine waking up every morning to a view of the sparkling Mediterranean Sea. If that is your dream, you should take a closer look at coastal regions like Cala d'Or or Port d'Andratx. These areas are known for their luxury properties and exclusive ambiance. But beware, exclusivity comes at a price. However, remember that the best investment is the one in yourself! Perhaps you prefer the authentic Mallorca life? Then places like Sóller or Pollença are just right for you. Here you can enjoy the local culture to the fullest and settle down in one of the charming village houses or renovated fincas. Let the tranquility of the mountains and the warmth of the locals enchant you.

Or are you more of the active type, seeking adventures and a dynamic environment? Then Palma is your go-to! As the bustling capital, Palma offers not only a wide range of properties, from modern apartments to historic palaces, but also an exciting nightlife and diverse cultural offerings.

The square meter prices indicated in the statistics naturally include all existing properties. Therefore, these prices do not solely focus on high-end living space. For this reason, I would like to mention prices from my experience that may appear more realistic for your project. No matter where on the island, the best properties are also the high-priced offers. Please consider that in all the different urbanizations and regions of Mallorca, prime locations differ in price from B-locations. Of course, there is a gradient, which I will explain in this chapter.

Let's start in the much sought-after southwest of the island!

The Southwest Coast of Mallorca:

Sun, Beaches, and Luxury

The southwest coast of Mallorca is undoubtedly one of the most coveted and exclusive regions of the Balearic Island. Known for its dreamy beaches, luxurious resorts, and excellent cuisine, this coastal region attracts visitors from all over the world. In this detailed text, we will explore the highlights and charm of the southwest coast of Mallorca more closely.

Dreamy Beaches:

The beaches of the southwest coast of Mallorca are among the most beautiful in the world. Cala d'Or, Cala Portals Vells, and Playa de Palma Nova are just a few of the paradisiacal beaches that can be found here.

With their fine sand and crystal-clear waters, they are perfect for sun worshippers and water sports enthusiasts. Water skiing, sailing, snorkeling, and diving are very popular here. The beach of Es Trenc, often referred to as Mallorca's "Caribbean beach," stretches over eight kilometers and is a true dream beach.

Marinas and Water Sports:

The southwest coast of Mallorca is a paradise for sailors and yacht owners. In the exclusive marinas of Puerto Portals and Port Adriano, you will find an impressive collection of luxury yachts and a vibrant scene with exquisite restaurants, trendy bars, and designer boutiques. Water sports such as jet skiing, sailing, and windsurfing are very popular here. Port Adriano, designed by Philippe Starck, is an architectural gem that also hosts art exhibitions and cultural events.

Excellent Cuisine:

The southwest coast of Mallorca offers an excellent culinary scene that will satisfy even the most demanding gourmets. In Santa Ponsa, Port Andratx, and other coastal towns, you will find a variety of restaurants led by Michelin-starred chefs serving culinary delights from Spanish and international cuisine. Be sure to try the fresh seafood and fish dishes, accompanied by top-class Mallorca wines.

Golf Paradise:

The southwest coast of Mallorca is also a paradise for golfers.

The region is home to some of the island's finest golf courses, including the renowned Santa Ponsa Golf Club, which hosts international tournaments.

The breathtaking scenery and mild climate make playing golf here a pleasure throughout the year.

Cultural Highlights: Although the southwest coast of Mallorca is primarily known for its luxury and beaches, there are also some cultural treasures to be discovered. The picturesque village of Andratx features a charming old town with narrow streets and historic buildings. The church of Sant Elm offers a stunning view of the nearby island of Sa Dragonera and is well worth a visit.

The southwest coast of Mallorca is undoubtedly one of the most glamorous regions of the island and synonymous with luxury and elegance. Here you can enjoy the sun, experience the best beaches, taste the finest cuisine, and experience the exciting nightlife. Whether you're looking for a romantic getaway, a luxurious retreat, or simply an unforgettable stay, the southwest coast of Mallorca will fulfill all your desires.

The southwest consists of the capital Palma to the municipality of Andratx. It includes the city of Palma de Mallorca, the municipality of Calvia, and the municipality of Andratx. And it is located at the foot of the Tramuntana Mountains.

The southwest enjoys the greatest attention from interested parties. It impresses with the best developed infrastructure. On the one hand, the capital Palma and the airport can be reached in just a few minutes by car.

As the capital of the Balearic Islands, Palma de Mallorca, with its approximately 470,000 inhabitants, is also the cultural center of the island. For this reason, proximity to Palma is highly sought after and is often used primarily for visits in the autumn, winter, and spring.

On the other hand, the southwest has prepared itself for year-round use. Property owners particularly appreciate that they can not only supply themselves with shopping throughout the year but also find the best restaurants open. Likewise, doctors, banks, etc., are based here and are available throughout the year as well.

The southwest impresses with international flair and lifestyle. There are also climatic differences worth mentioning. It is somewhat cooler here in the summer months. This difference amounts to about 2 to 3 degrees Celsius. However, with the high temperatures, it is a noticeable difference.

In the winter months, it is slightly warmer in the southwest. Here too, the difference is about 2 to 4 degrees, which contributes to well-being. The reason for this is the Tramuntana mountain range. The strongest winds and bad weather fronts mainly hit the island from the north and west. Therefore, the Tramuntana Mountains protect the southwest of Mallorca from these weather influences.

Here, the prices are the highest. Unsold living units start at around 4,000 euros per square meter. These units are usually then renovated. Through high-quality renovation, these prices can be raised to approximately 7,000 to 9,000 euros. Living units in prime locations quickly reach 10,000 euros per square meter. However, square meter prices beyond 15,000 euros are not uncommon. Nonetheless, you also get a lot for your money.

The West Coast of Mallorca:

An Oasis of Peace and Natural Beauty

The West Coast of Mallorca, also known as the "Costa de Tramuntana," is a region of unparalleled beauty and tranquility. Away from the hustle and bustle and the tourist hotspots that characterize the island, the West Coast offers an authentic, picturesque, and natural setting that is perfect for escaping everyday life and experiencing the true essence of Mallorca. In this detailed text, we will explore the highlights and peculiarities of the West Coast of Mallorca.

The Serra de Tramuntana:

The West Coast of Mallorca is dominated by the impressive Serra de Tramuntana, a mountain range that has been declared a World Heritage Site by UNESCO.

This majestic mountain range stretches along the entire northwest coast of the island and offers some of the most breathtaking landscapes in Mallorca. The Serra de Tramuntana is a paradise for hikers and nature lovers, providing a wealth of trails that wind through lush forests, picturesque villages, and along steep cliffs. Here, you can enjoy the tranquility of nature and be enchanted by the beauty of the mountain scenery.

The Picturesque Sóller:

The village of Sóller, located on the West Coast of Mallorca, is a true gem of the region. Known for its charming architecture, cobblestone streets, and Mediterranean flair, Sóller is a popular spot for visitors who want to experience the authentic side of Mallorca. One of the main attractions in Sóller is the historic tram that connects the village with the Port of Sóller, offering a scenic ride through orange and olive groves. The Jardí Botànic de Sóller, a botanical garden, is also worth a visit, housing an impressive collection of Mediterranean plants.

The Picturesque Port of Sóller:

The Port of Sóller is an idyllic place that's perfect for a relaxing day by the sea. With its small fishing boats, waterfront cafes and restaurants, and sandy beach, the Port of Sóller is a favorite destination for travelers who want to enjoy the peace and beauty of the West Coast. A nostalgic tram connects the Port of Sóller with the village of Sóller, and a historic railway line runs from Sóller through the Serra de Tramuntana to Palma.

Cultural Treasures:

The West Coast of Mallorca also harbors some cultural treasures. In Valldemossa, a picturesque mountain village, you can visit the former Carthusian Monastery La Cartuja, where the famous composer Frédéric Chopin and writer George Sand spent some time. Today, the monastery serves as a museum providing insights into the life and work of these artists.

Culinary Delights:

The West Coast of Mallorca is renowned for its excellent cuisine. In local restaurants, you can savor fresh seafood, traditional Mallorca dishes such as "Tumbet" (a vegetable casserole) and "Sobrassada" (a spicy sausage), as well as delicious orange products from the region. The restaurants near the Port of Sóller are particularly known for their fresh fish dishes.

The West Coast of Mallorca is an unparalleled destination perfectly suited for nature lovers, hikers, culture enthusiasts, and travelers looking to experience the true soul of Mallorca. With its breathtaking landscape, picturesque villages, and rich culture, the West Coast is a true oasis of tranquility and beauty on this stunning Mediterranean island.

The West Coast refers to the towns in the Tramuntana Mountains. The most renowned places are certainly Valldemossa, Deià, and Port Sóller. Here, one experiences the most spectacular sunsets with endless views of the sea. On clear days, you can discern the silhouette of Ibiza. Along the steep cliffs of the Tramuntana Mountains, one primarily finds small coves, many with pebble beaches.
Exceptions like sandy beaches are rather rare here. Among these exceptions is the beach of Port Sóller.

The atmosphere of the West Coast is special. Over centuries, farmers created numerous terraces to cultivate their crops. Olive groves and citrus tree plantations line the streets here. The Tramuntana Mountain Range is part of the UNESCO World Heritage and impresses with its lush nature.

However, in terms of the real estate market, this also means that building land is extremely scarce. Occasionally, there are one or two plots of land available for construction within the various urbanizations in the mountains, but these are then offered at absolute premium prices. Even on the West Coast, prices ranging from 4,000 euros to beyond 15,000 euros per square meter are achieved.

The Northwest Coast of Mallorca:

A Paradise for Nature Lovers and Explorers
The Northwest Coast of Mallorca is a unique gem on the popular Balearic Island, offering a fascinating mix of breathtaking nature, historic villages, and picturesque coastal towns.

Away from the overcrowded tourist paths, this region attracts visitors who want to experience the authentic side of Mallorca. In this detailed text, we will take a closer look at the highlights and unique beauty of the Northwest Coast of Mallorca.

Stunning Coastal Landscape:

The Northwest Coast of Mallorca impresses with its dramatic coastal landscape. Along this coast, you'll find spectacular cliffs, hidden coves, and crystal-clear waters.

Cape Formentor is a prominent feature known for its stunning views of the sea and surrounding mountains. The bays of Cala Sant Vicenç and Cala Deià are perfect spots for a relaxing day by the sea and offer top-notch opportunities for snorkeling and swimming.

The Serra de Tramuntana:

The Northwest Coast of Mallorca is dominated by the majestic Serra de Tramuntana, a mountain range that has been classified as a World Cultural Heritage site by UNESCO. This impressive mountain chain stretches across the entire Northwest Coast of the island and offers numerous hiking and trekking opportunities. Here, you can enjoy breathtaking views of the coast, deep ravines, traditional villages like Deià and Valldemossa, as well as unique flora and fauna. The hike from Sóller to Port de Sóller through the Valley of Oranges is one of the most popular routes in the region.

Culture and History:

The Northwest Coast of Mallorca is rich in culture and history. The village of Valldemossa is famous for its former Carthusian monastery where the renowned composer Frédéric Chopin and writer George Sand spent some time.

Today, the monastery serves as a museum providing insights into the lives and works of these artists. The village of Sóller is also a cultural highlight, with its Gothic cathedral and the historic tram that connects the village with the Port of Sóller.

Culinary Delights:

The Northwest Coast of Mallorca offers a wide range of culinary delights. In the coastal towns and villages, you will find numerous restaurants serving fresh seafood, traditional Majorcan dishes such as "Tumbet" (a vegetable casserole) and "Sobrassada" (a spicy sausage). The region is also known for its almond trees and almond products, which you can find in many local shops.

The Northwest Coast of Mallorca is a versatile and fascinating destination that is equally attractive to nature lovers, hikers, culture enthusiasts, and those seeking relaxation. With its stunning coastal landscape, historic villages, and rich culture, the Northwest Coast is a true gem on this beautiful Mediterranean island. Visit this region and let yourself be enchanted by its unique beauty and charm.

Upon arriving in the Northwest, you encounter the towns of Pollença and Alcúdia. From Pollença, you can reach the northernmost tip of the island, known as Cap Formentor. Puerto Pollença is located right at the large Bay of Pollença and invites kite surfers to enjoy their sport due to the high wind strengths.

Next to it lies the town of Alcúdia with its beautiful historic center. There, you can also visit the first Roman settlement.
At about 3 kilometers, on one hand, you have one of the most beautiful golf courses in Spain, Alcanada. A short distance from there is Puerto Alcúdia and the tourist-utilized part of the town.

Even in this area, there are properties that reach the square meter prices of the Southwest. However, it is rather the exception. But please do not assume that there are special offers to be had.

Here, too, you will find square meter prices between 4,000€ and 7,000€. The only difference is that the number of properties that exceed these prices is smaller. In terms of property size, very large properties are less common here. More often, apartments and somewhat smaller houses or fincas are on offer.

These are indications that the purchase prices tend to be more favorable. The slightly lower prices are since this area is not specialized for year-round use. On the other hand, this zone offers a more authentic Mallorca experience. However, personal life provisioning during the winter months is somewhat more complicated; on the other hand, you are surrounded by lush nature and much tranquility.

Particularly the towns of Pollença and Alcúdia are almost closed during the winter months, so you must travel a bit further for shopping and social life.

The North Coast of Mallorca: A Paradise for Nature Lovers and Explorers

The North Coast of Mallorca, also known as "Costa Nord," is a unique and fascinating area of the popular Balearic Island.
Away from the mass tourism that characterizes the South Coast, the North Coast offers a quieter and more authentic side of Mallorca. In this detailed text, we explore the beauty and attractions of the North Coast.

Spectacular Coastal Scenery:

The North Coast of Mallorca impresses with its dramatic coastal landscape. Along this coast, you will find steep cliffs, hidden coves, and crystal-clear waters. The Bay of Pollença and the Bay of Alcúdia are two of the most renowned coastal areas, offering perfect conditions for swimming, snorkeling, and water sports. A boat trip along the coast is a fantastic way to admire the impressive rock formations, such as the Cap Formentor.

The Serra de Tramuntana:

The North Coast of Mallorca is dominated by the majestic Serra de Tramuntana, a mountain range that has been designated as a World Heritage Site by UNESCO.

This impressive mountain range extends across the entire northwest coast of the island and offers numerous hiking and trekking opportunities. Here, you can enjoy breathtaking views, visit historic villages like Deià and Valldemossa, and discover the unique flora and fauna of the region.

Cultural Treasures:

The North Coast of Mallorca is also home to some notable cultural treasures. In Valldemossa, a picturesque village nestled in the mountains, you can visit the former Carthusian monastery La Cartuja, where the famous composer Frédéric Chopin and writer George Sand once lived. The monastery is now a museum, offering insights into the lives and works of these artists.

The Charming Alcúdia:

The historical town of Alcúdia, situated on the North Coast, is another highlight. It enchants visitors with its well-preserved city walls and the narrow, cobblestone streets. In the old town of Alcúdia, you'll find an abundance of restaurants, shops, and traditional markets. Visit the weekly market to purchase local products such as fresh fruit, vegetables, olive oil, and handmade crafts.

Culinary Delights:

The North Coast of Mallorca is also a paradise for food connoisseurs. Try fresh seafood, traditional dishes like "Frito Mallorquín" (a hearty meat and vegetable stew), and the local specialty "Sobrassada" (a spicy sausage) at the local restaurants. In the villages of the Serra de Tramuntana, you will find cozy restaurants serving traditional dishes in picturesque settings.

The North Coast of Mallorca is a region of unparalleled beauty and authenticity. Here, you can escape the hustle and bustle, experience nature in all its glory, discover cultural treasures, and savor the island's culinary delights. Whether you are a hiker, beach lover, or cultural enthusiast, the North Coast of Mallorca has something to offer for everyone and will captivate you with its unique atmosphere and charm.

The North Coast is characterized by very small villages and is very quiet during the winter months. Behind the coastal villages lie beautiful Mallorca villages surrounded by stunning finca countryside. The landscapes here are gently rolling but tend to be rather flat, with gorgeous panoramic views sometimes stretching out to the sea. Here, one can still find the authentic Mallorca away from the large holiday destinations.

Prices there start at around €3,000 per square meter of living space. The real estate on offer mainly consists of apartments and smaller villas and fincas. However, properties with a significantly higher price per square meter also exist here. This area is more suited to the individual-oriented customer.

Those seeking tranquility and wishing to avoid crowds will find themselves very well-positioned here. Due to the geographical arrangement of the Mallorca villages up to the coastal towns, the infrastructure is more extensively developed. Here too, to manage daily life and obtain groceries, one must be prepared to travel greater distances.

The East Coast of Mallorca: An Oasis of Beauty and Diversity

The East Coast of Mallorca is a true gem of the Balearic Island, attracting thousands of tourists from all over the world each year. Known as the "Costa de Llevant," this region offers a fascinating mix of breathtaking natural beauty, picturesque villages, historical sights, and vibrant coastal towns. In this detailed text, we will explore the highlights and unique features of Mallorca's East Coast.

Enchanting Beaches:

The East Coast of Mallorca is renowned for its spectacular beaches. One of the most famous is undoubtedly Cala Millor Beach, a miles-long golden sandy beach that is perfect for sunbathing and swimming. Cala Millor also offers a variety of water sports, including sailing, windsurfing, and diving. Equally impressive are the coves of Cala Agulla and Cala Mesquida, surrounded by untouched nature and crystal-clear waters.

"Weighing up your lifestyle, it's purely a matter of taste where you find your wedding mobile on Mallorca. This island offers so much and is simply magical..."

Nature's Paradise:

The East Coast of Mallorca is characterized by a diverse natural environment. The Parc Natural de Llevant nature reserve extends over much of the region and offers hikers and nature enthusiasts numerous opportunities to discover Mallorca's unique flora and fauna. Here you will find Mediterranean forests, impressive cliffs, secluded coves, and breathtaking sea views. The park is also home to a variety of animal species, including wild goats, eagles, and many rare birds.

Picturesque Villages:

The East Coast of Mallorca is dotted with charming villages that offer visitors a glimpse into traditional Mallorcan life. The village of Artà is an outstanding example with its narrow streets, historic buildings, and an impressive market held every Tuesday.

In Capdepera, visitors can explore the well-preserved fortress of Castell de Capdepera, which offers a breathtaking view of the coast. The village of Sant Llorenç des Cardassar is known for its agricultural tradition and picturesque squares where one can fully enjoy the local life.

Historical Treasures:

The history of the East Coast of Mallorca is rich and varied. In addition to the fortresses and historical buildings that adorn the region, the archaeological site of Son Real is also worth a visit. Here, visitors can explore prehistoric tombs and remains of a Roman settlement. Another highlight is the Basilica of Sant Salvador in Artà, a Gothic church from the 13th century that is not only an impressive religious structure but also offers a great view of the surrounding landscape.

Culinary Delights:

The East Coast of Mallorca offers a wide range of culinary delights. In the coastal towns, you will find numerous restaurants serving fresh fish and seafood.

The traditional Mallorcan cuisine is also well represented here, with dishes like "Tumbet" (a vegetable casserole) and "Sobrassada" (a spicy sausage). Do not forget to try "Ensaimadas" in the local bakeries, a sweet pastry that is extremely popular on the island.

The East Coast of Mallorca is a diverse and fascinating destination that has something for everyone. Whether you want to explore natural beauty, discover historical treasures, or simply relax on the beach, this region has it all. Set out to explore the Costa de Llevant and be enchanted by its beauty and diversity.

Throughout the entire East Coast, we find many smaller towns with their romantic and picturesque coves. This creates a unique atmosphere that can only be found in this number on the East Coast. Likewise, scattered along the entire East Coast are sports and yacht harbors that attract not only ship owners but also locals and tourists to enjoy the lifestyle and flair, as well as the local gastronomy.

Apart from a few exceptions, here one can also enjoy the more original Mallorca. The properties mainly on offer are apartments and smaller villas. Since the entire East Coast consists of significantly flatter land than the West Coast, where the Tramuntana Mountains are located, there are many finca offerings due to the topography.

Here, properties with smaller unit sizes and somewhat more affordable prices per square meter are offered, with real estate prices starting at around €3,000 per square meter. However, for top-location properties, prices can go up to €10,000 per square meter. Nonetheless, the offering in this price segment is manageable.

The Southeast Coast of Mallorca:

A Paradise of Nature and Tradition

The Southeast Coast of Mallorca, also known as "Costa de Levante," is a charming and diverse region of the Balearic Island. Away from the crowded tourist areas, this coastal region offers a unique blend of unspoiled nature, picturesque villages, and cultural heritage. In this detailed text, we will explore the highlights and charm of the Southeast Coast of Mallorca.

Natural Beauty:

The Southeast Coast of Mallorca is characterized by a breathtaking natural environment. A standout feature is the Mondragó Natural Park, a protected area with an impressive landscape of Mediterranean forests, coastal cliffs, turquoise bays, and pristine beaches. Here, nature lovers can hike, bird-watch, and admire the indigenous flora and fauna. Another gem is Cala Sa Nau, an idyllic cove with crystal-clear water, perfect for snorkeling and swimming.

Charming Villages:

The villages along the Southeast Coast of Mallorca exude an authentic Mallorcan charm. The village of Santanyí is famous for its elegant stone houses, its vibrant weekly market, and the impressive Parish Church. Cala Figuera is a picturesque fishing port known for its characteristic boathouses that stretch along the harbor basin. In Felanitx, you can visit the impressive Church of Sant Miquel and the Monastery of Sant Salvador.

Cultural Treasures:

The Southeast Coast of Mallorca is also rich in cultural heritage. Visit the Santuari de Sant Salvador Monastery in Felanitx, which sits atop a hill and offers an impressive view of the surroundings. The Castell de Santueri fortress is another historical highlight, providing insight into the island's tumultuous history. The village of Porreres is known for its traditional handicrafts and wine production.

Culinary Delights:

The Southeast Coast of Mallorca boasts a rich culinary tradition. In local restaurants, you can enjoy traditional dishes such as "Tumbet" (a vegetable casserole), "Frit de Matances" (a meat dish), and the local sausage specialty "Sobrassada". The wineries in the region also produce excellent wines, which you can try during a tasting.

Traditional Festivals:

The Southeast Coast of Mallorca is also known for its traditional festivals and events. The Fest of Sant Jaume in Santanyí and the Fest of Sant Miquel in Felanitx are just two examples of the vibrant celebrations that focus on local culture and tradition. These festivals offer a great opportunity to experience the Mallorca way of life and taste local specialties.

The Southeast Coast of Mallorca is a region rich in natural beauty and cultural heritage. It offers an ideal setting for nature lovers, hikers, and travelers who want to discover the quieter side of Mallorca. With its picturesque villages, historical sites, and delicious culinary delights, the Southeast Coast of Mallorca is truly a magical part of the island.

The Southeast of Mallorca stretches from the municipality of Santanyí to Llucmajor. Mainly, you will find very beautiful fishing villages with their sports and yacht harbors as well as very picturesque small coves for swimming. Adjacent to this is the nature-protected Es Trenc beach with its dune landscape.

Inland, various Mallorca villages are surrounded by finca developments. The municipality of Llucmajor then borders the city of Palma. Here too, square meter prices start at around 3000€. Offers with significantly higher square meter prices are also available in smaller numbers. As with the previously described zones, smaller housing units are typically offered here as well, which is why more affordable offers can also be found. From the Southeast, you can reach the airport in a timely manner.

The South Coast of Mallorca:

Sun, Beaches, and Diversity

The South Coast of Mallorca, also known as "Costa de la Luz," is one of the most popular and lively regions of the Balearic Island.

This coastal region is known for its sunny Mediterranean climate, its breathtaking beaches, its vibrant holiday resorts, and its diverse cultural heritage. In this detailed text, we will explore the highlights and charm of the South Coast of Mallorca.

Beaches and Coves:

The beaches along the South Coast of Mallorca are undoubtedly some of the bests on the entire island. The beach of Playa de Palma stretches for several kilometers and is a popular spot for sun worshippers and water sports enthusiasts. Here, you will find a variety of water sports opportunities, from jet skiing to windsurfing. Nearby is also the beautiful natural beach Es Trenc, known for its fine sand and crystal-clear water. Cala Pi and Cala Blava are charming coves surrounded by impressive cliffs and are perfect for peaceful days by the sea.

Cultural Treasures:

The South Coast of Mallorca also has several cultural treasures to offer. The capital, Palma de Mallorca, is a cultural hub with a rich history. The impressive La Seu Cathedral, the historic Castell de Bellver, and the charming district of La Lonja are just a few of the attractions to be discovered in Palma. The city also has a vibrant art scene with museums and galleries, including the Es Baluard Museum for Modern and Contemporary Art.

Party and Nightlife:

The South Coast of Mallorca is also known for its lively nightlife. The holiday resorts of Magaluf and El Arenal are particularly famous for their party atmosphere. Here you'll find an abundance of bars, clubs, and discos where you can dance the night away. Magaluf's Beer Street is a well-known hotspot for partygoers. However, it should be noted that the party scene is mainly limited to certain areas, and the region also offers quiet and family-friendly zones.
Culinary Delights:

The South Coast of Mallorca offers a wide range of culinary delights. In the coastal towns, there are numerous restaurants that serve fresh fish and seafood. Also, try the Mallorcan paella, a delicious rice dish with various ingredients such as chicken, seafood, and vegetables. The tapas bars are another highlight for tasting local specialties.

Nature Reserves:

The South Coast of Mallorca also provides access to some impressive nature reserves. The Mondragó Natural Park, located near Santanyí, is home to unique flora and fauna as well as beautiful hiking trails and coves. Here, you can experience the untouched nature of Mallorca.

The South Coast of Mallorca is a diverse and vibrant region that has something to offer everyone. Whether you want to enjoy the sun and beaches, delve into the island's culture and history, or experience the exciting nightlife, this region has it all. Discover the South Coast of Mallorca and let yourself be enchanted by its beauty and variety.

The South Coast of Mallorca stretches all the way to our capital, Palma de Mallorca. The airport is just a few minutes away, and the capital itself is only about a 20-minute drive. On the one hand, there are many finca (rural estate) offers here, and as one gets closer to Palma, more tourist hotspots begin to emerge, where you mainly find smaller housing units and apartments.

Here, the real estate stock is of an older vintage, so one must expect to pay around 3000€ per square meter for properties that have not been renovated. Renovated and like-new properties in the top locations already described also reach square meter prices of about 10000€.

The Central Mallorca:

A Diverse Heart

The center of Mallorca is a fascinating and often overlooked part of the Balearic Island, offering a rich mix of natural beauty, cultural heritage, and authentic Mallorca lifestyle. In this detailed text, we will explore the various facets and attractions of Central Mallorca.

Rural Idyll:

The center of Mallorca is characterized by its rural and often untouched landscape. Here you will find gentle hills, lush olive groves, vineyards, and picturesque villages that are perfect for relaxing walks and bike rides. This area of Mallorca has largely been spared from mass tourism, thus providing a peaceful escape from the bustle of coastal resorts.

Historic Villages:

In Central Mallorca, there are numerous historic villages worth visiting. Sineu, for example, is known for its traditional Wednesday market, which is considered one of the oldest on the island. There, you can buy local products, handicrafts, and culinary specialties. Alaró is another charming village near the Tramuntana Mountains with a well-preserved castle that offers breathtaking panoramic views.

Cultural Heritage:

Central Mallorca is rich in cultural heritage. The Santuari de Cura monastery on the Randa Mountain is a spiritual center that has attracted pilgrims and visitors for centuries. The impressive Basilica of Santa Maria del Camí is a masterpiece of Gothic architecture and a significant religious building on the island.

Wine Production:

Central Mallorca is also known for its wine production. The region around Santa Maria del Camí is a center for viticulture, where you can taste some of the best Mallorcan wines. Numerous wineries offer tours and tastings, where you can discover the secrets of Mallorcan winemaking.

Culinary Delights:

Central Mallorca offers an authentic culinary experience. In the villages and towns of the region, you'll find cozy restaurants and tapas bars serving traditional Mallorcan dishes.

Try "Lechona" (suckling pig), "Frito Mallorquín" (a hearty stew), and "Sobrassada" (a spicy sausage), accompanied by local wine and fresh bread.

Natural Beauty:

Central Mallorca also hosts some natural beauties. The Parc Natural de Mondragó offers hiking trails through forests and along the coast, as well as the opportunity to explore pristine coves and beaches.

Central Mallorca is a diverse and often overlooked part of the island that holds many treasures for travelers who want to experience the quieter and more authentic side of Mallorca. From rural idylls to historic villages to culinary diversity, Central Mallorca offers a rich palette of experiences for every taste. It is the ideal place to dive into the soul and heart of this beautiful Mediterranean island.

The central part of the island is distinguished exclusively by its village and finca life. From the center of the island, you can reach the capital Palma in about 20 to 25 minutes by car. Naturally, housing units with a sea view are scarce here, if at all, they are very distant. The center of the island has its own atmosphere. The Mallorca village and finca life is often still very original and authentic.

Here, as in the previously described zones, square meter prices start at about 3000€, but you can also find luxurious housing units priced up to 10000€ per square meter. Individualists will feel very much at home here too.

Palma de Mallorca: The Shining Capital of the Balearics

Palma de Mallorca, the capital of the Balearic Islands, is a vibrant hub for culture, history, nature, and modern life on the beautiful island of Mallorca. This city harmoniously combines the treasures of a rich past with the conveniences of a modern metropolis. In this detailed text, we will explore the diversity and charm of Palma de Mallorca in greater detail.

History and Culture:

Palma de Mallorca has a long and eventful history that is reflected in its architecture and cultural heritage. The city's landmark is the majestic Cathedral La Seu, a masterpiece of Gothic architecture. Its striking structure stretches along the shore of the Bay of Palma and impresses visitors with its tall towers and intricate stained-glass windows.

The Castell de Bellver is an imposing fortress from the 14th century, perched high above the city offering breathtaking panoramic views. The Old Town of Palma, also known as "Casco Antiguo," is a charming labyrinth of narrow streets, historic buildings, and cozy squares. Here you will also find the royal palace Palau de l'Almudaina, an impressive Moorish castle.

Shopping Paradise:

Palma de Mallorca is a shopping paradise for fashion enthusiasts and souvenir collectors. Passeig del Born and Avinguda Jaume III are bustling shopping streets with a variety of boutiques and stores where you can find fashion, jewelry, and crafts. Mercat de l'Olivar is a lively market where you can purchase fresh food, spices, and local delicacies. Here, you can also experience the rich culinary diversity of Mallorca.

Beaches and Coasts:

Although Palma de Mallorca is a city, it still offers access to beautiful beaches and coves. Playa de Palma is the city's most famous beach and stretches over several kilometers. Es Trenc, known as Mallorca's "Caribbean Beach," is just a short drive from the city and is distinguished by its fine white sand and turquoise waters. The seaside promenade Paseo Marítimo along the Bay of Palma is a popular spot for walks and features a variety of restaurants and bars.

Gastronomy:

The gastronomic scene of Palma de Mallorca is first-class. The city boasts an impressive selection of restaurants offering local and international cuisine. Try fresh seafood, authentic Mallorca dishes like "Paella" and "Tumbet," accompanied by a glass of local wine. The up-and-coming neighborhood of Santa Catalina is known for its trendy restaurants and bars serving modern cuisine and creative cocktails.

Culture and Events:

Palma de Mallorca offers an abundance of cultural events and festivals throughout the year. The international film festival "Evolution Mallorca International Film Festival" attracts cinephiles from all over the world.

The city festival "La Nit de l'Art" is an art exhibition that transforms the city streets into an open-air museum. The festival "Festes de la Mare de Déu de la Salut" in August and the procession "Sant Sebastià" in January are festive highlights in Palma's calendar.

Palma de Mallorca is an exciting and diverse destination that offers the perfect balance between tradition and modernity. Whether you want to explore rich history, relax on the beach, shop, or enjoy culinary delights, this city has something for everyone. Immerse yourself in the fascinating world of Palma de Mallorca and let yourself be enchanted by its charm and diversity.

The capital of the Balearic Islands dazzles with its vibrant rhythm and cosmopolitan life. It is undoubtedly the cultural center of the Balearic Islands. Particularly in the historic old town, the international clientele is interested in purchasing real estate. The prices per square meter for unrestored living space are approximately €4,000, while for renovated living space, peak prices reach approximately €15,000 to €20,000 per square meter.

The previously described square meter prices in the individual zones should, of course, only be seen as indicative. Even within these zones, as elsewhere, there are prime locations as well as secondary ones. The accessibility of each zone is just as much a part of the explanation for the different square meter prices that are established.

In recent years, large four-lane exit roads have been built from Palma to the areas I described earlier. For this reason, these areas can now be reached within 45 minutes by car. Since then, these areas have become increasingly attractive to many prospective buyers. Of course, the much sought-after southwest of the island remains the area with the best infrastructure and is also the only area that has been geared for year-round use.

However, the significantly higher purchase prices for residential units in the southwest are not only due to a somewhat higher price per square meter but also due to a more spacious and therefore larger number of square meters per residential unit. For this reason, many of my international clients choose the southwest.

If the twelve-month orientation and proximity to the capital, Palma, are not of paramount importance, one will also be able to find stunningly beautiful properties in other areas of the island. Of course, Mallorquins and now residents who naturally need to cater to themselves have been living there for centuries.

Having the capital Palma nearby and enjoying the international flair of the southwest does not have to be the right choice for everyone. For this reason, I recommend seeking extensive advice and possibly also looking for your dream property there. Ultimately, beauty is always in the eye of the beholder.

I personally love the island of Mallorca in each area and am sure that it will be easy for some to find their dream property in an area they have not yet considered.

Choosing the perfect place is crucial for your satisfaction and happiness on the island. Therefore, you should take your time to explore different regions before making your decision. Do not forget, each region has its own secrets to discover and cherish. Do not worry, you cannot go wrong, because Mallorca is an island that has something for everyone. Whether it's peace and seclusion or hustle and bustle and activity, Mallorca has it! The first step on this incredible journey is taken, and the possibilities are endless. Dream big because in Mallorca, dreams come true. You deserve it!

So, pack your bags and embark on this exciting adventure. Your dream property in Mallorca is waiting for you, and you are ready!

3.2. Top Regions and Their Advantages

Welcome to another fascinating section that will refine your idea of the perfect property in Mallorca. This time we take you on an exciting tour through the top regions of the island and their advantages, so you can optimally plan your investment.

Let's start with the stunning southwest coast. Places like Andratx and Portals Nous are synonymous with glamour and luxury. Here you can relax on world-class golf courses, anchor your yacht, and enjoy exquisite seafood in Michelin-starred restaurants. This area is made for those seeking a touch of exclusivity.

But perhaps it is the originality that makes your heartbeat faster. Then you should not miss the Tramuntana mountains. In places like Deià or Valldemossa, you can feel the charm of bygone times, surrounded by the rugged beauty of nature. This is your chance to own an authentic piece of Mallorca that has already inspired artists and writers.

Or how about the east of the island? Areas like Cala d'Or and Porto Cristo offer wonderful beaches and idyllic coves. Life here is relaxed but far from dull. These places are ideal for families or couples looking for quality and tranquility without forgoing amenities.

Of course, we must not forget Palma, the heart of the island. As a cosmopolitan center, Palma has everything one could desire art, culture, history, and unbeatable infrastructure. For investors looking for a solid capital investment, the properties here are particularly interesting.

So, dear reader, the ball is now in your court. Each of these regions offers unique opportunities, and each has its own treasures. The fact is, wherever you invest, you are investing in a piece of paradise.

Let this information sink in because the decision you make will enrich your life like never before. Take the leap, dive into the diversity of Mallorca, and find your personal treasure. Believe in yourself and your dreams; it is in your hands! So, what are you waiting for? Mallorca opens the doors to a world full of possibilities. Seize them!

3.3. Hidden Treasures: Lesser-Known Regions

Have you ever wondered about the hidden gems Mallorca has to offer off the beaten path? Then this subchapter is tailored for you! We open the door to Mallorca's lesser-known regions that offer equally fascinating investment opportunities.

Let's start in the north of the island, far from the tourist crowds. Pollença and Alcúdia are two pearls that offer both cultural experiences and stunning nature. Nestled between mountains and sea, this is the ideal choice for those who crave peace and adventure at the same time. And the best part? Property prices are comparatively moderate here.

Further inland, we come across Sineu, known for its traditional weekly market. The vibrant heart of authentic Mallorca! With its rural fincas and charming village houses, this region offers a unique opportunity to invest in a piece of real Spain without sacrificing 21st-century comforts.

Or perhaps you are drawn to the southeast of the island? Santanyí is a gem that you should not miss. The relaxed atmosphere and the picturesque beaches that are not yet overrun by tourists make this area an ideal place for those who long for peace and authenticity.

Finally, let's not forget the west, where villages like Banyalbufar or Estellencs capture the hearts of their visitors by storm. Nestled into the slopes of the Tramuntana mountains, these places offer not only spectacular views but also a unique opportunity to acquire a sustainable property that stands in perfect harmony with the surrounding nature.

So, dear readers, now you know some of the hidden treasures that Mallorca has to offer. Each of these regions is unique and could be the perfect home for your next great adventure.

Now is the time to set sail and explore the unknown. Dare the first step and discover places that exceed your wildest dreams. Your courage will be rewarded—with a life in one of the lesser-known, but no less enchanting, corners of this magnificent island. The choice is yours; you have the power. Seize it!

3.4: The Importance of Location and Its Impact on Price

It is a phrase that is repeated so often in the real estate industry that it almost sounds cliché: "Location, location, location." But this phrase is much more than just a cliché; it's a wisdom for anyone wanting to invest in the fascinating world of real estate. You have the power to choose the perfect location for your dream project on Mallorca. But how exactly does location affect the price? In this subchapter, you will find out exactly that!

Let's start at the coast. The magical attraction of the sea naturally drives prices up. If your dream property offers a view of the deep blue Mediterranean, be prepared to pay a premium price. But rest assured, the investment is worthwhile! These properties are not only beautiful but also extremely stable in value.

Well, what about the charming villages inland? While they may not offer the same panoramic views, they have their own allure. Here, the prices are often lower, yet the potential for appreciation is enormous, especially as tourism and infrastructure continue to grow.

The capital, Palma, is a chapter. A bustling hub of culture, nightlife, and economy, where prices can vary greatly depending on the district. A luxury apartment in the old town district can easily cost twice as much as a similar property in a less sought-after quarter. But here too, investing in a good location pays off in the long term.

And let's not forget the mountains! The Tramuntana region offers spectacular views and a unique way of life. Prices can be quite high here due to limited availability and high demand. Yet, if you are looking for a retreat that offers both seclusion and exclusivity, this is where you'll find it.

Ladies and gentlemen, the choice of location is a decision with far-reaching implications, not only for the price but also for the quality of your life on Mallorca. It's in your hands to make the right choice for your budget, your needs, and your dreams. And every place you choose has its own special potential. Trust your intuition and let yourself be inspired by the countless possibilities that this enchanting island has to offer. Now is the time to enrich your life with an investment as individual as you are!

3.5. Mallorca Real Estate, What to Consider?

What follows is a very interesting chapter. The right real estate expert in Mallorca by your side will naturally be happy to enlighten you about this. Ultimately, it is a decision that you must make for yourself because it should always revolve around your comfort experience. To fully enjoy your dream property, you should be aware of the type of lifestyle property you want to acquire.

The undoubtedly most important elements of a property are always the location, the location, and the location again! Intensive consulting and the associated explanation should be at the beginning of all considerations. In the previous chapter, I briefly explained the peculiarities of the individual areas. Once you have decided on an area, the decision is made as to what type of property it should be. It will seem very simple to you whether you want to acquire an apartment, a villa, or a country house.

An apartment is certainly the easiest to manage. Here, you are only responsible for the care and maintenance of the interior spaces. The communal area in residential complexes is maintained by the community and assigned with the monthly housing allowance, also called monthly apportionment.

Apart from apartments or flats in residential complexes, there are also houses in community complexes, known as "gated communities". It all depends on the statute of the community complex, whether the available private

In case the community does not maintain the garden, the owner must organize it individually.

If you dream of a detached villa, the maintenance of the entire property must be organized individually. The monthly charges saved must therefore be invested in service companies. There are many property management companies on the island that will gladly take care of this. However, finding trustworthy companies is unfortunately a challenge. If you do find a real estate expert who provides comprehensive support, you will certainly be able to rely on their network.

The property requiring the most maintenance, however, is the finca, or country house. It's a very beautiful and romantic notion to enjoy nature on your finca. However, one must be aware that a finca is very labor-intensive. The maintenance and upkeep are significantly more demanding. This is because the soil on the island is very fertile. Everything grows at a rapid pace and must be constantly kept under control. Accordingly, a larger amount must be allocated for maintenance to secure your investment. Of course, it should be noted that any property can only maintain or ideally increase its value if it is well-kept.

The question of whether to buy an old building or a new construction depends on the condition of the old building. Since the 1980s, properties have been built using what is known as skeleton construction. This means that a reinforced concrete skeleton is poured, which is then filled with masonry.

Therefore, there are no load-bearing walls. This means that renovation is easier to carry out. It is worth mentioning that a house built in skeleton construction is extremely stable and solid. The advantage for you is that on the second attempt you can create your custom-made suit. However, this also assumes your willingness to engage in renovation or refurbishment at all.

The first goal should always be to find a dream property that is ready to move into. Of course, it also always depends on having the right real estate expert by your side to be able to make these final decisions.

The most complex option is to decide on a building plot or land. Anyone who chooses this option should be aware beforehand that after the purchase, planning and preliminary work must be pursued intensively. Here too, you need an experienced real estate expert by your side who can introduce you to a standardized process.

Let's assume that you have found the right building land for yourself. Together with your real estate expert, two important cornerstones of the project must now be committed.

First, the right architect must be researched. In the first planning phase, you will work closely with this architect. He will design your dream house and take your ideas into account as fully as possible.

Parallel to this point, the technical architect must be engaged. From my perspective, perhaps even the most important figure, since the technical architect, also known as the Aparejador, controls the technical implementation and represents your interests. The right Aparejador is directly commissioned by you and is accountable only to you. He oversees the correct execution and ensures the construction quality by certifying each stage of the construction progress.

He carries out this supervision in close collaboration with the architect. Only after the technical architect's certification can subsequent partial payments be made to the various recipients. It is advisable to hire an independent technical architect. For new constructions as well as extensive renovations, both the architect and the technical architect are legally required.

It is recommended to place project management in experienced hands. There are also individual solutions for this. If you have already won a real estate expert who has the experience and has earned your trust, they might be the right choice. However, this position can also be filled by your technical architect.

If you have now filled the key positions for your project and the planning phase is complete, the implementation begins. When asked about the timeline, it is unfortunately difficult to provide a blanket answer. During the tourist season, between Easter and the end of October, various municipalities restrict which construction activities are allowed. The aim is to protect holidaymakers from being disturbed by excessive noise. Take, for example, the municipality of Calvia in the southwest of the island. Between May 1st and October 31st, noisy construction activities are restricted. During this time, loud machinery may only be used between 10:00 a.m. and 1:30 p.m. For 3.5 hours a day, construction companies are unable to provide their personnel and machinery.

This means that the completion of a project is significantly extended. Therefore, please assume that the completion of your project will take between 18 and 24 months. Not to forget the prior planning time. After the architect has submitted the project for approval to the municipality, the official building permit is granted after approximately 6 months. From this, you can see that you need to calculate approximately 24 to 30 months for the completion of your dream property. In addition, you must be aware that even the best team cannot keep every difficulty at bay.

The advantage of a new build lies in two essential points. First, you are creating your custom fit. Second, you gain a financial advantage compared to the acquisition of a turnkey property. Despite these two advantages, most clients opt to purchase a finished property and thus avoid the higher time investment. It is advisable to search for a finished object and accept the slightly higher purchase price first thoroughly. Rest assured; your dream house is already waiting for you!

4. Purchase Process and Important Advice

4.1. Mallorca Real Estate: What to Consider When Buying?

So, you've decided to acquire your dream house in Mallorca. Excellent choice! But as with any significant decision, the details matter. A well-planned purchase process can mean the difference between a fantastic investment and a disappointment. We'll guide you through the most important steps to ensure your property purchase in Mallorca is a complete success.

Let's start with the preparation phase. You need a budget, and this budget should be realistic. Try to estimate the total costs, including additional purchase costs and any renovation work, to avoid unpleasant surprises.

But money isn't everything. Your investment should also be emotional. Consider what exactly you expect from your property in Mallorca. Whether you want to enjoy the sun or escape the hustle and bustle of everyday life – always keep your desires and needs in view.

Now onto documentation. Ensure that all documents are complete and up to date. This includes not only the land register extract but also proof of the proper payment of taxes and fees. Also, check for any encumbrances or restrictions. A reputable real estate agent can help you with this.

The most important documents must now be presented to ensure that the property meets all legal requirements and is habitable. Without these documents, the purchase is legally ineffective.

Choosing the right notary and the suitable real estate expert is also crucial. You want partners by your side who are not only competent but also trustworthy. Do not compromise; your investment is too valuable for that.

Finally, the actual purchase process: You sign the preliminary contract and pay a deposit into the notary's account. At the notary appointment, the deed is authenticated, and the balance becomes due. Now the keys are handed over, and the immediate transfer of ownership occurs. Congratulations, you are now the proud owner of a property in Mallorca!

See, the process doesn't have to be complicated if you are well-prepared. Take the time to carefully plan and execute each step. Your future self on the sun-drenched porch of your dream home will thank you. Make your dream come true now!

4.2. The Safest and Fastest Method to Your Dream Property

If you've decided to purchase a property in Mallorca, you've already taken the first brave step into a wonderful, exciting future. Now, you undoubtedly want this process to be as smooth and swift as possible without compromising on security. And this is indeed possible!

First and foremost: Get informed. Knowledge is the most powerful weapon in any purchasing process. Do your research, seek expert advice, and exchange information with other property owners. This way, you create a solid foundation for the upcoming decisions.

Then, rely on professionalism. An experienced and competent team of real estate experts, lawyers, and notaries is indispensable. These professionals can identify pitfalls that you as a layperson might overlook. Their expertise helps you save time and money and ensures that everything is in order.

As for financing, you should consider various options. Be proactive and clarify your financial situation in advance, perhaps even before you start looking at properties. This way, you know exactly what is within your budget and can act immediately when you find your dream home.

But what's the fastest method to find that dream property? Your individual Mallorca real estate expert! Through their network, such as local contacts or expat groups, you benefit from important sources of information. They know the island and can provide valuable insider tips.

So, if you follow the recommendation and fill this key position with your individual Mallorca real estate expert, you will be able to not only obtain your dream property as quickly as possible but also safely and pleasantly. The explanations have repeatedly pointed out certain conditions to you.

1. Find your real estate expert who will advise you individually and intensively on the Mallorca real estate market.

2. Your real estate expert will create your requirement profile together with you.

3. Your real estate expert searches specifically and individually for you across the entire Mallorca real estate market for optimal properties.

4. Your real estate expert presents you with suitable and pre-checked properties that match your requirements profile.

5. All presented properties are personally known to your real estate expert.

6. You decide in consultation with your real estate expert which properties should be viewed.

7. You decide on your dream property.

8. Your real estate expert will take over the price negotiation with you in consultation.

9. After successful price negotiations, your real estate expert prepares the private purchase contract.

10. The legal review of the property records is carried out.

11. Your real estate expert plans and organizes the notary appointment and presents all necessary documents and certificates to the notary.

12. The notary prepares the notary appointment and sends the draft for review to you or your real estate expert.

13. On the agreed date, the completion and conclusion of the purchase process take place with the signing of the notarial purchase deeds, simultaneous transfer of funds, handing over of keys, and thus the immediate transfer of ownership.

14. Congratulations! You are now the owner of your dream property in Mallorca.

15. Your real estate expert will then carry out all necessary registrations and deregistrations and hand over a worry-free package to you.

Another tip for speed and security: Once you have found your desired property, do not hesitate. In a booming market like Mallorca, hesitation often means losing out. Make a serious offer and secure the property with a deposit.

Finally, the topic of contract design should be mentioned. A clearly formulated and balanced contract protects your interests and makes the entire process more secure. Be thorough and do not let yourself be rushed. Your personal Mallorca real estate expert will accompany you competently and reliably.

In summary, your success is determined by a combination of good preparation, the right support, and swift action. You hold the reins for a secure and fast transaction in your hands. Act wisely, and your dream of owning a property in Mallorca will become a reality sooner than you think!

4.3. Overview of Additional Purchase Costs

You should not underestimate the additional purchase costs because these can either facilitate or complicate the path to your dream property in Mallorca. But don't be discouraged! With the right knowledge and necessary planning, additional costs are just another hurdle to be skillfully overcome.

- Initially, you should know that additional costs usually amount to about 10-12% of the purchase price. Yes, that is a considerable sum, but think of the bigger picture: the value and joy that your new property will bring.

- The property transfer tax is one of the most significant items. In Mallorca, it varies between 8% and 13%, depending on the value of the property. Ensure you have budgeted for this amount. After all, you don't want any nasty surprises.

These additional purchase costs are one-time expenses. However, you will have ongoing costs in the form of taxes, community charges, and utility costs. I will discuss these in detail in the following chapter. The additional purchase costs thus refer solely to the acquisition of your new dream property and are as follows: The purchase of a used property is subject to property transfer tax (ITP). In the Balearic Islands, the following property transfer taxes apply when buying a used property:

- the first €400,000 of the purchase price is taxed at 8%
- between €400,000.01 and €600,000, the property transfer tax is 9%
- the amount between €600,000.01 and €1,000,000 is taxed at a rate of 10%
- the purchase price between €1,000,000.01 and €2,000,000 is taxed at 12%
- the purchase price over €2,000,000.01 is taxed at 13%.

Example calculation with a purchase price of €1,200,000:
- up to €400,000 tax burden 8% = €32,000
- for the amount between €400,000.01 and €600,000 is 9% = €18,000
- on the amount from €600,000.01 to €1,000,000 is 10% = €40,000
- on the amount from €1,000,000.01 to €1,200,000 is 12% = €24,000
- Total taxes amount to €114,000 The tax is to be paid within 30 days after the transfer of ownership.

 Notary fees and land registry fees are additional, typically around 1-2% of the purchase price.

If a lawyer is consulted, they would charge additional fees amounting to 1 to 2% of the purchase price. It is, of course, the buyer's prerogative to hire a lawyer. Your trusted advisor can also recommend a lawyer to you.

While the purchase of a used property is subject to property transfer tax, the purchase of a new-build property is subject to Value Added Tax (IVA). The applicable tax rate depends on the type of property: for residential properties including garage spaces (maximum 2 per dwelling unit), 10% IVA is payable on the purchase price. For the purchase of land from a commercial enterprise as well as the purchase of commercial properties, the tax rate is 21% IVA. Either property transfer taxes or VAT are payable, never both taxes together.

As a private buyer, the outlined additional purchase costs cover the valid rates for most buyers. However, there are special situations, such as in the case of gifts or inheritance, which have their own specificities that make individual consultation indispensable. The costs for the real estate agent are usually included in the purchase prices since the agent is paid by the seller's side. Make sure you have clarity about these fees from the beginning.

Another important point is administrative costs. These include, among other things, the transfer of utility contracts and could amount to a few hundred euros. Minor in comparison to the other items, but not to be neglected.

What about renovation or modernization? These costs are optional but can be significant depending on the condition of the property. Plan generously because nothing is more inspiring than the opportunity to design your new home to your own specifications.

Now that you have an overview, it's time to create a detailed cost summary. This will help you keep track and focus better on the search for your dream property.

Be not only brave but also wise. A thoughtful plan will bring you closer to your dream property and give you the feeling of security and satisfaction that you have everything under control. Don't let additional purchase costs act as an obstacle but as an incentive to be even better prepared. And then, dear readers, nothing stands in the way of your dream!

Here again, the exclusive cooperation with your personal real estate expert Mallorca pays off, who can advise you comprehensively.

4.4. Annual Taxes and Fees for Property Owners

You've made it, the dream property in Mallorca is now your home or your perfect vacation destination. While the journey there was full of tension and challenges, don't forget that every investment comes with a responsibility. However, this is no cause for concern but another step on your exciting journey.

Annual taxes and fees can be a surprise for some, but not for you, because knowledge is power! You are already working with your Mallorca real estate expert, so you are informed about these items.

In addition to the additional purchase costs, there are also other ongoing taxes and fees. The property tax, locally known as "IBI," is probably the most prominent item. It is paid to the respective municipality and usually ranges between 0.4% and 1.1% of the cadastral value. The good news is that this value is often lower than the market value. Who wouldn't want to save on taxes while enjoying the sun of Mallorca?

The property tax (IBI) is levied on the value of rural and urban land based on the cadastral value by the competent municipality and is due annually.
During the financial crisis, many municipalities had drastically increased property tax.

In the Balearic Islands, the property tax is calculated by multiplying a certain factor by the cadastral value and relating it to the building. The exact values can be provided by the municipal administration upon request. Compared to the value of the property, this tax is relatively low.

Non-resident property owners are required to pay income tax. The Spanish tax authorities' tax the benefit of self-use as fictitious rental income for a non-resident who uses the property only for vacation purposes. The tax is 19% on 1.1% of the cadastral value. But don't worry, with good tax advice, this hurdle is easy to overcome.

Example calculation:
Cadastral value €380,000 1.1% of €380,000 = €4,180 on that 19% = annual income tax €794.20 The cadastral value does not correspond to the market value. This value is significantly below the market value.

That means in the example described above, the market value of the property with a cadastral value of €380,000 is probably closer to €800,000 to €900,000.

Sewer fees and garbage collection are other annual costs. Although they are low compared to other items, it is still advisable to include them in the budget. Because every journey, including the one into the world of real estate in Mallorca, consists of many small steps.

In addition, community fees may apply, especially if your property is part of a larger complex with common facilities such as a pool, garden, or security services. These fees vary widely but often offer excellent value in the form of carefree living.

You see, owning a property in Mallorca is more than just a one-time purchase. It is a lifelong relationship that requires attention, care, and yes, also financial resources. But like any good relationship, it is worth the effort. With this knowledge, you can confidently dive into your new chapter.
Your dream property is waiting not only to be purchased but also to be loved and cared for by you. And you are well prepared for it!

5. The Right Partner: Real Estate Agents in Mallorca

5.1. The Importance of a Real Estate Agent in Purchasing

One of the critical factors that can make the difference between a smooth and a problematic real estate experience is the choice of the right real estate expert.

Imagine navigating the maze of real estate purchasing with an expert by your side. Someone who knows the pitfalls and can guide you safely through the process. In this subchapter, we will explain exactly why a good real estate agent is indispensable for your investment in Mallorca.

A real estate expert is not just a salesperson; they are an advisor, a negotiator, and often a psychologist. They have the experience and market knowledge to guide you through decision-making. The agent can help you find the right location for your budget and needs because they know the island like the back of their hand!

A qualified real estate expert can save you not only time but also money. Think about the negotiations that will likely take place. An agent can remove emotions from the process and ensure that you get the best price for your dream property. Furthermore, they can assist you in handling all formalities, from drafting a purchase agreement to handing over the keys.

But that's not all. A good real estate expert has a broad network of contacts: from notaries and lawyers to architects and craftsmen. So, you can be sure that every detail is in the best hands.

Exclusive cooperation with an independent real estate expert in Mallorca is recommended. This expert will manage the local process for you and mediate between the provider, like an agent, or directly with the property owner, and you. This service does not trigger any additional costs for you.

You might wonder if you should really invest in an agent. The answer is a resounding yes! Since the agent's commission is paid by the previous owner of the property, it is already included in the purchase prices. See it as an investment in your well-being and financial security. Your personal real estate expert in Mallorca will not only help you find the right property but will also contribute to your long-term enjoyment of your investment.

So, take the initiative and make the first step on your way to your dream property in Mallorca. Look for your personal real estate expert in Mallorca who shares your values and vision. You are just a few steps away from beginning a new chapter in your life on this beautiful island, and a personal real estate expert in Mallorca can be your faithful companion on this exciting journey!

5.2. Selection Criteria: Which Real Estate Agent is Right for Me?

When stepping into the fascinating world of Mallorca real estate, one person plays a special role: your personal real estate expert in Mallorca.
A knowledgeable, trustworthy expert can be the key to your dream property. But how do you find the expert that really suits you? In this subchapter, we will take a closer look at this question.

Experience is, of course, an important factor. A real estate expert with years of practice not only knows the market but also the nuances of the negotiation process. However, don't be dazzled by the number of years alone. Pay attention to how well the real estate expert understands your specific needs and desires. Good communication is key to a successful partnership.

Networking is another criterion. A good real estate expert is well-connected and can provide you with valuable contacts to financial experts, lawyers, and craftsmen. A broad network is often a sign of trustworthiness and quality in the industry.

Also, look for online reviews or personal recommendations. Satisfied customers are the best advertisement, and testimonials can give you an initial impression of what to expect. But don't just rely on the words of others; meet potential real estate experts in person or in a video call and form your own opinion.

Another important point is the specialization of the real estate expert. Are they specialized in the type of property you are looking for? Whether it's luxury villas, apartments, or country houses – a specialized real estate expert will be better able to meet your specific needs.

Lastly, you should also keep an eye on the fee structure. Transparent, fair fees are an indicator of a real estate expert's seriousness. And remember good work has its price, but it can save you a lot of money in the long run.

However, the most important thing is to listen to your gut feeling. Do you feel comfortable with the real estate expert? Do they understand what you are looking for, and can you trust them? If all signs point to yes, then congratulations: you have found the partner who will accompany you on your journey to your dream property in Mallorca. Don't miss this opportunity and embark on the adventure that will delight you for a lifetime!

5.3. Recommendations and Pitfalls in Searching for a Real Estate Agent

You have already learned a lot about the criteria that are important when choosing a real estate agent. Now we would like to guide you through the recommendations and possible pitfalls that you should consider when searching for an agent on the magical soil of Mallorca.

Starting with the recommendations: If you have several agents shortlisted, don't hesitate to compare them directly. From the initial consultation to the range of services offered, this can help you make an informed decision. A little tip: ask the agent for references and look at completed projects. A proven agent will be proud to show you, their successes.

Now to the pitfalls: Beware of agents who demand excessively high fees or try to rush you into a quick conclusion. A reputable agent will always give you the time you need to make a well-informed decision. Even if some offers may seem tempting, haste is rarely a good advisor.

Another pitfall could be the lack of clarity about fees. A transparent agent will disclose all costs from the beginning. If fees are hidden or only revealed late in the process, that's a red flag.

And as for recommendations, look for a real estate expert who offers a holistic service. This means they provide support beyond the purchasing process, whether in legal advice or in arranging property management services.

Remember, the chemistry must be right. Even if all the boxes are checked, a good personal relationship with your agent will make the entire process not only more pleasant but also more efficient.

The search for your real estate expert is your first stop on an exciting journey that could culminate in owning a wonderful Mallorcan property. Take the time to make the right choice, because this decision will lay the foundation for your future happiness.

And rest assured: The perfect property, complemented by the perfect partner, will give you a sense of freedom and satisfaction that is priceless. For the reasons described above, collaboration with your personal real estate expert in Mallorca is recommended, which protects you from certain contingencies. So, embark on this adventure – Mallorca is waiting for you!

5.4. Benefits of Professional Real Estate Services

You've worked through the economics, the regions, and even the pitfalls and recommendations. Now you might be wondering: Why should I even consider a professional real estate agent? Here are the answers that will not only dispel your skepticism but also excite you for the unparalleled benefits of professional mediation.

First: Expertise. An experienced real estate expert in Mallorca knows the market inside out. You get valuable insights into price developments, location advantages, and hidden risks. You save not only time but also nerves. The real estate expert in Mallorca will guide you through the complex bureaucratic processes, so you can focus on what's essential: your future dream property.

Second: Negotiation skills. A real estate expert in Mallorca is not only a guide but also a skilled negotiator. They can influence the price in your favor and negotiate conditions you may not have even thought of. Your financial leeway is optimally exploited, and you acquire your property under the best conditions.

Third: Network and contacts. A real estate expert in Mallorca has access to a broad network, ranging from the construction company to the notary. You benefit from preferred conditions and sometimes even get access to properties that are not yet publicly on the market.

Fourthly: Emotional Distance. Buying a property is not only a financial but also an emotional affair. A real estate expert in Mallorca maintains the necessary professional distance and helps you make well-informed decisions, free from emotional impulses.

Fifthly: After-Sales Service. A good real estate expert in Mallorca will not abandon you once the contract is signed. They assist you with the handover, with renovation work, or with finding suitable tenants if your property is an investment.

Consider the real estate expert in Mallorca as your personal assistant, navigator, and advisor all in one. With the right partner at your side, the process of buying a property in Mallorca becomes not only easier but also more enjoyable. So, seize the opportunity! Let's embark on this journey together. Mallorca is waiting to be discovered – and you could soon be part of this Mediterranean paradise!

5.5. How do I find my dream property most safely and quickly?

In the following chapter, I would like to give you a serious and objective overview. With my 25 years of know-how, I want to convince you of what I consider to be the most efficient process. Over the years, I have been able to gain extensive experience and notice that many customers lose sight of the goal somewhat. The mentioned goal should be to enjoy the available time in one's dream property with loved ones and friends.

The Mallorca real estate market is characterized above all by its lack of transparency. Over 90% of the available properties are mediated through real estate agents. There are about 1000 real estate agencies in Mallorca with about 6000 employees. Furthermore, these properties are generally offered on the market.

This means that a property owner can collaborate with all distributors. For this reason, you will find the same property listed with many different providers. Coming from your home country, you may be accustomed to the idea that a property is exclusively distributed by one agent. This alone is a significant difference that is responsible for a lack of transparency.

To get as much information as quickly as possible, you naturally use the internet. There you usually search with mobile devices at any time of the day or night for real estate offers. These property offers are of course provided immediately. From the point of view of receiving this information and thus being able to make a pre-selection, the internet is a great medium. But please be sure to consider that this does not verify the seriousness and authenticity of the offers.

 These property offers can be found on relevant real estate portals, as well as on the websites of individual real estate providers or real estate agents. However, this does not guarantee that the published offers correspond to reality, or have been sold long ago, let alone ever existed. The offers on the portals are unfortunately only rudimentarily maintained and do not guarantee availability.

In the portals, both private and commercial providers offer properties. Likewise, the quality of the information is unchecked. Square footage details are not comparable to the usual net specifications. The number of rooms always refers only to the number of available bedrooms. In many different property portals, individual real estate companies are free to publish their offers. This is why you can find the same property offered by different real estate agents.

Now the question arises, which real estate agent should you contact to get more information? Of course, there are very good and reputable real estate companies in Mallorca. Unfortunately, this market is very uncontrolled, and anyone could register their business. I write about this so openly and transparently because it is also a thorn in the side of my well-known, very good, and very serious partner companies.

Especially in recent years, there has been a real flood of companies that spring up like mushrooms. Most of these companies disappear from the market after a few months. The dream of selling real estate in Mallorca and becoming a millionaire in the following 12 months is usually the biggest incentive.

These young companies massively underestimate how much professionalism, seriousness, competence, know-how, and diligence must be invested to be able to survive in the Mallorca real estate market in the long term.

The competence of a real estate agent is to be able to inform you about tax and legal issues. However, the real estate agent is not allowed to provide tax and legal advice. There are specialists for that. The competence primarily lies in fundamentally knowing the property offered. This means that the agent has personally visited each of his listed properties, has listed them in his portfolio, and therefore can tell you all the advantages but of course also all the disadvantages.

Most of my colleagues are very reluctant to do the groundwork. In the company where I learned my craft, the requirement was to personally know all listed properties to be able to advise the customer comprehensively. This is the absolute foundation to submit the right offers to the customer.

The agent must primarily be able to listen well and put the needs of his customer at the center of his activity. He must also ask the right questions. Only then does the customer's profile develop, and the agent is enabled to find and/or offer the right property. This working method distinguishes the professional from the amateur. Choose the professional right away. He will save you a lot of time, energy, and financial effort and enable you to enjoy your property as quickly as possible.

The Mallorca real estate market is an internationally oriented market that operates completely contrary to the standard real estate market in the home country. Most customers do not live on the island or in the next town and can appear spontaneously for viewings. Pre-planning is therefore essential and sometimes takes months.

Additionally, the customer must be advertised internationally. This is a significant financial challenge for every successful company. Many new companies fail precisely because of this. Unfortunately, this also affects the quality. Most of them unfortunately do not have the appropriate training or expertise to be called professionals. These 1,000 existing official companies with their approximately 6,000 employees are only the tip of the iceberg. Sometimes we get the feeling that every waiter, every receptionist, or other non-industry employees are also real estate agents. This is not conducive to achieving higher provider quality.

For this reason, I am convinced that one of the biggest difficulties is finding the right individual real estate expert. As already mentioned, property offers are available 24 hours a day. It is a veritable flood of information. However, having access to information does not make one a Mallorca real estate expert. As already mentioned, there is a real flood of agents. However, the quality of training leaves much to be desired.

From the home market, we are accustomed to properties being offered exclusively. Now, viewing appointments are made with as many different real estate agents as possible. Since you have already learned that here you must resort to a general market, you now know that the individual properties are offered by various agents. This automatically leads to the fact that most of the appointments could have been saved because the properties are often also offered by the previous agent.

If the goal is clearly defined, namely, to find and enjoy your dream property, you should put yourself in trustworthy hands and let a professional do the work. However, you have the great advantage that you only must open to one real estate expert and secondly, that this real estate expert works individually for you and compiles various offers that fit your profile and searches individually for you.

Another big disadvantage of working with too many agents is that the agent is usually only interested in showing you as many properties as possible. The reason for this is the legal situation. Only the agent who personally presents a property to you is the only agent entitled to a commission. After a viewing, you are registered by name with the owner, which is the legal basis for any commissioning. Of course, only in the case of actual purchase, but you will therefore also see properties that are not of interest to you.

Countless interested parties have therefore often flown home frustrated in the past because they have seen too much. And what they have seen did not fit their inquiry profile.

To achieve the optimal goal, the path there should also be as pleasant as possible because it may also be fun. After all, one is not looking for their dream property every day. For many of my customers, this is a long-cherished dream that is now to come true. A seven-figure investment is quickly reached, and for this reason, one should choose the best procedure.

5.6. Which Real Estate Agent is Best for Me? Which real estate agent is right for me?

These are questions that are becoming increasingly important for many clients, as it's easy to lose sight of the forest for the trees due to the large number of agents. In fact, however, it is also one of the most important questions and decisions one faces. Most of the island's properties are mediated through real estate agents. But the best real estate agent doesn't have to be the largest provider. The best real estate agent is the one who puts you at the center of the action and focuses on your wishes.

Of course, it can be an agent who works for a large company. Unfortunately, this is not automatic. Large companies often require their employees to work according to a certain scheme. If this scheme is successful, it will continue to be pursued in the future. This could be the right scheme for you. However, an individual working method is rather the exception.

There are also very good agents who either work in smaller companies or alone. Here, too, one can find the right partner. Unfortunately, smaller companies usually do not have a meaningful portfolio. However, this has nothing to do with an unprofessional method of working, but simply with the temporal difficulty of obtaining an extensive portfolio.

It is recommended to have an independent real estate expert in Mallorca who will implement your dream with you. Above all, he should enjoy your trust and convince you with his competence and seriousness. Offer you his entire expertise, including his entire network.

Advise you without calculating his commission in advance and stand by you honestly, transparently, and seriously.

Mutual sympathy naturally completes the process. However, since it also involves a high investment for you, you need a real estate expert who also protects you from wrong decisions. A wrong decision could be, for example, to absolutely want to sell you the most expensive property, although a slightly cheaper one perfectly fits your profile. Or failing to explain all the negative aspects of a property and concealing any illegality.

So, if you find a real estate expert who deals with you in the described honest, transparent, and serious manner, that could be the right partner for you. Ultimately, you decide how you want to experience this entire process and what you want to spend your money on. However, it should lead to few problems finding your property with the mentioned cornerstones. This will bring you closer to your dream and reach it quickly!

Also, your real estate expert should invest their time individually and intensively. Implementing your dream can go very quickly, but unfortunately, it can sometimes take a little longer. Therefore, your real estate expert should always keep you up to date on the timing and explain the various market conditions to you.

The Mallorca real estate market operates by its own rules. The law of supply and demand has a special significance here. The demand for properties in Mallorca is continuously very high.

The optimal real estate expert should naturally only show you properties that match your request profile. Many agents do not listen carefully to their clients and show too many properties that do not fit the client's request profile.

Therefore, you need a competent, transparent, and serious real estate expert who can create your request profile and can therefore offer you optimal properties. Even with this quality alone, you save a lot of time and get closer to your dream quickly. This quality of your real estate expert should be the basis to meet your standards at all. Beyond this foundation, he must have extensive experience and expertise on the island. Only if he has a significant network will he be able to offer you the best properties from various providers.

Nevertheless, he must have personally visited any property he offers you. Only then will he be able to advise you comprehensively on these offers. So, he must do his homework for you. He should be a proven expert in the Mallorca real estate market and have learned and understood the business from various perspectives.

Your request profile includes the type of property, the style of the property, the location, and of course, the size and the amount of the investment you are aiming for. But that's only the first part. The next step is about the quality of the materials used and the quality of the entire property. For this, extensive experience is needed, which only a specialist from various areas of the Mallorca real estate market can provide. The use of materials alone is a comprehensive topic.

If you like to surround yourself with natural materials, you must understand that the maintenance effort is significantly higher. The climatic conditions in Mallorca are completely different from those in your home country. On average, there is a much higher humidity throughout the year. The significantly higher temperatures due to the intense sunlight in combination with the salty air put a much higher strain on materials in general.

You will understand that the right real estate expert for you in Mallorca must be able to do much more than just show you a property. With their help, you will find your dream property in a timely manner. You can already look forward to it!

6. Strategy for Buying Real Estate

6.1. Preparation and Planning: The Key to Success

Success doesn't happen by chance; it's the result of careful planning and tireless efforts. Imagine holding the key to your dream property in Mallorca. Can you feel the euphoria, the triumph? These moments are within reach, but only if you prepare correctly. In this subchapter, we will guide you through the crucial steps on the way to your dream property.

With this strategy, you will find and enjoy your dream property in the fastest and most effective way. For this, you need a personal attitude that focuses your attention on owning your dream property. The mere process of searching for the dream property should be a means to an end and not the center of attention. This immense time spent searching for the dream property should be done for you by a declared Mallorca real estate expert. Accordingly, you should focus on finding the right and professional partner for you.

The first step on this exciting journey is self-reflection. What do you really want? Is it a picturesque coastal house, a modern city apartment, or a rustic country house in Mallorca style? Clearly define your desires and needs, as this will be the guide for your entire real estate strategy.

Your real estate expert will advise you comprehensively and individually. He works exclusively for you and will develop your personal requirement profile together with you.

This profile consists of detailed information that enables your expert to search for the optimal dream property and compile a meaningful selection for you.

In this process, your real estate expert will clarify with you exactly which area in Mallorca is the optimal area for you. Whether it should be an apartment or a flat, or a house in a community complex. Perhaps a detached villa is the right choice. Another variant is the country house or estate, but perhaps the much described finca is the right choice. If you are looking for a turnkey property, you can use your dream property without further delay.

Of course, the market opens to a larger offer if you are also willing to buy a property in need of renovation. Your real estate expert will also be happy to advise you on the effort involved. The effort consists of two main points. First, how much time is involved? And secondly, how much is the financial effort. The advantage of such a project lies in implementing your own taste and personal preferences. Thus, you can create your so-called tailor-made suit.

Another very important point is which architectural style you prefer. Mallorca is certainly a hotspot in this respect as well, as many different styles have taken hold on the island. Renowned architectural firms have been looking for various influences around the world for many years, which they then implement here on the island. This is certainly one reason why Mallorca is known for its high exclusivity. Again, your lifestyle is at the center of attention, which is a very important part of your requirement profile.

Mediterranean Architecture: A Timeless Choice

Mallorca continues to be a bastion of Mediterranean architecture. This style has evolved over centuries and retains its relevance. The long, overhanging terraces provide shade in the summer, while the low-lying sun in winter reaches deep into the rooms. Additionally, Mediterranean architecture is characterized by smaller windows. This style is predominantly found in rural areas and fincas, but also in villa urbanizations with a Mediterranean elegance or manor house style. In rural areas, a more rustic variant is common.

Over the past 20 years, modern architecture has made its mark. Ultra-modern residential complexes for apartments and houses, as well as stately villas, are now the norm. Another wonderful trend is the creation of modern variants of Mediterranean architecture, leading to the contemporary design that has amassed a large following. I am a big fan of these designs, which bring Mediterranean architecture into the modern present. New buildings, as well as thoroughly renovated properties, meet the highest technical standards.

The Size of Your Dream Property: A Key Question

The size of your dream property is another key question to consider. The number of rooms offered always refers to the number of bedrooms. Apartments or flats usually ask for 2 to 3 bedrooms. It is important to note that not all residential complexes have basements or underground parking, due to the high construction costs associated with building basements on the island.

Mallorca has only about one meter of topsoil, underneath which is often rocky ground that makes excavation expensive. Those who have looked around Mallorca will have noticed the large diggers chiseling away at the rock in residential areas and villa urbanizations. This is why some customers opt for an extra bedroom right away.

For houses in complexes, as well as for detached villas or fincas, at least 3 bedrooms are preferred. Here too, I observe a trend towards 4 or 5 bedrooms. Through intensive discussions with your personal real estate expert, the image of what your dream property should look like and what it should offer to meet your lifestyle will crystallize.

The Most Important Characteristic of Your Dream Property: The Location of course, the location is the most crucial characteristic of your dream property. The location inevitably has to do with the chosen area where you want to spend your time. Whether it's the more authentic Mallorca with lots of peace and nature around you, or whether you also want to enjoy the international flair.

All these are important questions about your personal lifestyle. The decision on which location is the right one also includes whether you desire a sea view or prefer a view over lush nature. Perhaps the view is not your focus, but considering resale value, I can recommend from my personal experience to pay attention to the right location. In my view, it's the only guarantee for a quick resale.

Even if it doesn't currently align with your plans, holiday properties are typically resold after about 5 to 7 years. This is solely because your personal needs have changed. Perhaps you want to upsize or downsize. Maybe family and friends don't visit as often as you had hoped. Or maybe you no longer wish to live in a community complex and prefer to spend your time in your individual villa or finca. All of this can happen the other way around as well. However, one thing is also true: 95% remain loyal to the island and ultimately only change their lifestyle on our favorite island.

Yet preparation doesn't stop at choosing the perfect type of house. Financial planning is equally critical. Know your budget and consider all the additional costs that can accrue when buying property. Your creditworthiness plays a significant role, as do the economic conditions on Mallorca and interest rate developments. A prepared buyer is a successful buyer!

But the timing of the purchase can also be crucial. So don't wait too long, as prices on Mallorca continue to develop positively. Examine market trends and observe how prices in your preferred region have already evolved. Is there a chance for a bargain? Speaking of bargains on Mallorca certainly doesn't match a serious assessment. Or does everything indicate that prices will soar? Your timing could be the decisive factor that determines success or failure.

Let's not forget the role of experts either. Comprehensive preparation also includes choosing a qualified real estate expert in Mallorca, a trustworthy financial advisor, and an experienced lawyer. These experts are the pillars upon which your success rests. With a solid team by your side, you can avoid the numerous pitfalls that befall many buyers.

Even creating the requirement profile is associated with a lot of joy because you can talk openly about your real estate dreams with your real estate expert. In the first conversations, you will determine if your expert has the necessary expertise and if there is enough sympathy to be able to realize your dream through them. I can only recommend again and again that only the competent and serious real estate expert, who provides full transparency and all his know-how, is the most promising contact for the individual implementation of your project.

This expert has a network of other real estate professionals that has been tested over many years, which he manages and together with these experts presents the best properties that fit your project. This way, you receive a highly professionally prepared offer that has already been pre-checked for legality and gives you the assurance of being able to buy at the market-appropriate price/performance ratio.

Finally, it's about a substantial investment, and you want to be sure to pay a fair price for your dream property and not fall into the trap of buying at an inflated price. You can thus be assured of being able to enjoy this process relaxed, as your commissioned expert is exclusively available to you individually and does not have to follow the interests of the providers. The entire process must be designed to be as pleasant as possible for you and should protect you from unscrupulous offers, as all uncertainties have already been resolved for you.

Dear readers, the key to your dream property on Mallorca is in your hands. But let's be honest: It's a golden ticket you must earn. With the right preparation and a thoughtful plan, however, you stand at the gateway to paradise. And what could be more rewarding than that?

6.2. Market Analysis and Timing: When is the right time to buy?

Your dreams are within reach: you can almost smell the salty sea air of Mallorca and hear the gentle lapping of the Mediterranean. But as tempting as the prospect is, your decision must follow more than just an impulse. The perfect moment to buy a property is like a wave – it comes and goes, but if you catch it at the right moment, you'll enjoy a breathtaking ride.

Market analysis is your compass on this exciting journey. And the first step is to observe property prices and trends in your desired region. What factors influence the market? It could be economic indicators, seasonal fluctuations, or even political developments. Having a sharp eye on these factors can make the difference between a missed opportunity and a successful bargain.

But let's be realistic: Identifying the perfect timing is often challenging. Even experts can't always say with absolute certainty when the market has reached its peak or trough. But that's no reason to worry. You don't have to be perfect; you just need to be well-prepared. Tools like market reports, analysis, and your personal real estate expert are your guides through the complex landscape of the property market. Mallorca is a very price-stable and haven for your investment and has not been prone to price reductions so far.

Your timing should depend not only on the market situation but also on your personal life situation. Is your budget ready? Are your finances stable? If you are in a favorable position and the market presents you with your dream property, this could be your moment.

Remember: A well-timed property purchase is like an investment in a work of art – its value will increase over time, especially if you have made the purchase in a favorable market environment. Over the years, your house or apartment will not only become a home but also an asset that will increase in value far beyond the original price.

So, grab your chance by the forelock! Become the master of your own destiny and navigate skillfully through the tides of the real estate market.

Your dream of a property in Mallorca is not an illusion, but an attainable goal that is just waiting to be seized. And the key? The right timing combined with comprehensive market analysis. Let the dream become reality!

6.3. Financing and Budgeting

You stand on the brink of an adventure that can wonderfully transform your life. Financing your dream property in Mallorca is not just a matter of numbers but also of trust – trust in your financial capabilities and the strategic planning that has brought you here. First, it's crucial to clearly define your budget. How much can you afford without jeopardizing financial stability? Various financing options are available to you: from equity financing to mortgages and individual financing models tailored specifically for foreign buyers. The better you know your budget, the more targeted you can negotiate and maximize your leverage.

Financing is not just a dry exercise in mathematics. It is the heartbeat of your project that sets everything in motion. Consider which financing models fit your life situation. Talk to financial experts, take advantage of advisory services, and obtain offers from different banks. Your diligence now will pay off later in the form of a smooth financing process.

Don't forget the ongoing costs! Taxes, insurance, maintenance – all of this should be included in your budgeting. A well-thought-out financial plan enables you not only to afford the purchase price but also to fully enjoy life in your new property.

Your financial health is your strongest ally on this exciting path. And yes, there will be moments when the numbers and reality seem to resist. But remember that every milestone, every contract, and every financial decision brings you closer to your dream.

So be bold, but also wise. Be visionary, but also pragmatic. Your financial strategy is the key that opens the doors to a bright future in Mallorca. Trust in your abilities, your preparation, and your vision. In the right financing lies the magic that makes your dream come true. You have it in your hands!

6.4. Long-Term Considerations: Rental and Value Appreciation

You're on an exciting journey, and it's not just a short-lived affair. No, your decision to purchase a property in Mallorca is an investment in your future. And that's precisely why your focus should not only be on the here and now but also on what the coming years might bring.

Rental is a keyword you should keep in mind. Mallorca is a tourist magnet, and the demand for high-quality living space is constant. So, if you don't want to spend the entire year on the island, renting out your property can be a profitable source of income. But be careful! Successful renting requires more than just an available space. You need a solid strategy that also considers taxes, maintenance, and marketing.

Now, on to value appreciation. Every property in Mallorca has the potential to increase in value, especially if it is well-located and well-maintained. Here, small things can have a big impact. A kitchen upgrade, an attractive garden, or eco-friendly improvements can significantly increase the value of your property. You should always keep an eye on the market and trends to make the right decisions at the right time.

Your horizon should be broad, your vision clear. If you see your property not just as a roof over your head but as a living, growing part of your assets, then you are on the best path to maximizing your investment. The real estate market is like an ocean – deep, sometimes unpredictable, but full of opportunities. And you, equipped with the right strategy, can navigate these waters like a skilled captain.

You see, buying a property is not just a transaction, it's the beginning of an exciting, rewarding journey. A journey that, with the right planning and foresight, can enrich your life as well as your bank account. So set sail, your dream property in Mallorca awaits to become part of your long-term life and financial strategy. It's in your hands!

7. Results and Vision

7.1. The Path to Property Ownership: An Experience Report

Imagine opening the door to your new home in Mallorca, feeling the warming sun on your skin, and hearing the gentle murmur of the sea. Fantastic, isn't it? This vision can become a reality! You just must walk the path that countless successful property owners have trod before you. And the best part? This path doesn't have to be full of stumbling blocks. With the right information, the right partner, and a clear strategy, you will reach your destination faster than you might now imagine.

Every successful property purchase starts with a dream, but it's the implementation of this dream that really counts. The process can be lengthy and requires patience, attention, and careful planning. With a personal real estate expert in Mallorca, however, you will enjoy this process as quickly and pleasantly as possible. But the reward for all these efforts is priceless. Your own little paradise, a place where you can relax, recharge, and enjoy the finer things in life.

In retrospect, most property owners will tell you that there were moments of doubt and uncertainty. But they will also emphasize that the experience has made them stronger and that the insights they have gained are invaluable. Choosing the right real estate expert, understanding local laws and regulations, the intricacies of financing - all these things will become part of your armor, preparing you for future investments.

So don't just look at the immediate results. Your investment in a property in Mallorca is more than just a business; it's a life-changing experience. You're not just buying a house, you're investing in your well-being, your quality of life, your lifestyle, your family, and your future. This decision can enrich your life in ways that go far beyond the monetary aspect.

You've truly made it. Congratulations! Finally, as the owner of your dream property, you're affirmed in having made all the right choices. With the commitment of your real estate expert, you've come to enjoy your new lifestyle. The future time you'll spend in your dream property will increasingly confirm the significant enhancement of your quality of life you've created for yourself. You no longer must pack all your suitcases; from now on, just a little hand luggage will suffice, saving you stress and time on your travels.

Filled with happiness and pride in having made the right decision, you can now thoroughly enjoy everything with your loved ones, family, and friends. The search for your dream has now been fulfilled, and you no longer must constantly chase after it, but instead, live your dream with all your loved ones. The Mediterranean life!

Therefore, the message of this experience report is: Dare to do it! The path may seem challenging, but the rewards are worth it. Your dream of a property under the sun of Mallorca is within reach. And you have everything you need to make it a reality. Be courageous, be visionary, and above all, be yourself, because the adventure of your lifetime is just around the corner.

7.2. The Goals of Property Purchases in Mallorca

You have reached a magical point in your journey. The place where visions become tangible, and dreams are translated into reality. The property in Mallorca you have in mind is not just a place, but a symbol for numerous goals that lie behind it. But what are these goals, and how can they exponentially increase your quality of life? Let's unveil the mystery!

Firstly, there's the goal of quality of life. Owning a property in Mallorca means investing in a lifestyle characterized by sun, sea, and culture. Just imagine the countless sunrises and sunsets you can enjoy on your own terrace. Every time you open the door to your property, you're also opening a door to a better, more fulfilling life.

Then there's the financial goal. Mallorca has established itself as a stable and growing real estate market. An investment here is not just a place to live but also an opportunity for asset growth. In a world of uncertainty, a property on this beautiful island provides a solid foundation for your financial future.

Let's take it a step further and consider the goal of self-actualization. Owning a property is, for many people, a sign of success and independence. It's a manifestation of your hard work, smart decisions, and ambitions. Every time you welcome guests to your Mallorca home or enjoy the solitude of your own abode, you feel the triumph of self-actualization.

Not to forget the family goal. A property in Mallorca can be a family meeting point, a place where generations come together to create quality experiences and collect memories. It becomes a legacy that you can pass on, a solid constant in an ever-changing world.

You see, buying a property in Mallorca is not just a transactional act. It's a conscious step towards a multitude of goals that can enrich your existence in various ways. And it is here, in this chapter, that we want to assure you: your goals are tangible, achievable, and just waiting to be realized by you. Take the initiative, for the future belongs to the brave, and that could be you!

7.3. Long-term Perspectives and Value Development

Welcome to the heart of this life-changing adventure! If purchasing a property in Mallorca represents a meaningful chapter in the book of your life, then the concept of long-term perspectives and value development is the indispensable epilogue that completes a grand story. Here we encounter the invisible treasures that gain significance over years and decades.

Let's start with value development. Mallorca is not just an island of beauty but also of stability. The capital invested here grows not only through the natural appreciation of real estate but also through the continuous improvement of infrastructure and the growing attractiveness of the island. Your property will not only increase in value but also offer the potential to generate rental income. That's like a double gift waiting for you!

Now, to the long-term perspectives. Through this purchase, you are creating a legacy, a solid foundation for future generations. Your children and grandchildren will have not just a roof over their heads but also a space for creativity, happiness, and relaxation. The legacy is more than just material; it's emotional, its memory, it's family.

But it's not just about finances or inheritance. It's also about your long-term quality of life. Think of all the happy hours you will spend in your new home. About the relationships that will deepen, and the new friendships that will be formed. All this contributes to the quality of your life, in a way that cannot be measured with money.

Lastly, we talk about investing in yourself. By investing in a property in Mallorca, you invest in your dreams, your passions, and your peace of mind. It's a decision that says: "I deserve the best, and I'm ready to put it into action."

This subchapter is meant not only to inform but also to inspire. It should be a magnifying glass for your visions and a catalyst for your decisions. So do not hesitate! Use the incredible long-term perspectives and value development as a guide on your path to happiness. Because you deserve not just to dream, but to live your dreams.

7.4. The End of the Journey: The Dream of Mallorca Realized

You have made it. Let that sentence sink in for a moment. Breathe in the salty air deeply, feel the warm rays of the sun on your skin, and listen to the gentle murmur of the sea in the background. Your dream of owning a property in Mallorca is no longer an illusion – it has become a reality.

This is the moment to pause and congratulate yourself for the numerous challenges and victories that awaited you on this adventurous path. It has not been an easy journey, but the journey itself was already a win. And what you take away from it is far more than a physical structure of stone and mortar; it is a monument to your willpower, ambition, and dreams.

What comes next? A new chapter full of endless possibilities unfolds before you. Perhaps you already have plans for your new home. A garden full of Mediterranean plants, a cozy reading room, or a pool with a breathtaking view of the sea? The details are up to you, for this home is the blank canvas that you can now fill with the colors of your dreams.

The emotional and financial benefits of this realization will enrich your life in multiple ways. You will enjoy not only a sense of security and ownership but also see an investment that appreciates over time. Whether you decide to live in your new property or use it as a holiday home, the return is not only material but also spiritual.

This chapter may be the end of a journey, but it is certainly not the end of your dreams. It is rather a steppingstone for further adventures, further investments, and most importantly, more moments of happiness and contentment. Your vision has materialized, and the horizon is now clear and boundless.

Before we close this book, remember that every endpoint is also a beginning. A beginning to enjoy life to the fullest, with a new perspective and fresh energy to embrace all the challenges and joys that may still come.

Celebrate this victory. Take a deep breath. Look around. You have arrived. And this place, this feeling, is just a taste of the many wonders yet to come. Congratulations, you have earned it!

Conclusion and Outlook

You have reached the last page of this book, but the insights and inspirations you have taken away are much more than the end of this work. In the preceding chapters, we embarked on a journey that took us from the discovery of the magical island of Mallorca to strategic considerations and the realization of your dream. Yet, the journey does not end here. Instead, a new chapter of your life is just beginning.

With the tools you now possess, you are well-equipped to make your endeavor a success. Every word, every strategy, and every insight in this book was meant to inspire and encourage you, so that you can not only achieve your goal but also enjoy it.

The world of real estate in Mallorca is a dynamic ecosystem, constantly in flux. Ongoing developments offer both challenges and opportunities, but with your newly acquired knowledge and passion, you are ready to master both. Perhaps you are considering acquiring another property or seeing your newly acquired object as an investment opportunity. Maybe you want to share the experiences you've had on this path with others, thus sparking a wave of inspiration. The possibilities are endless.

Allow me to congratulate you on your determination and courage. The journey may have been arduous at times, but as you have seen, the journey is the reward. And the lessons you have learned along the way are invaluable.

In looking ahead, let's not talk about an end, but about a new beginning.

Mallorca surely has many hidden treasures and unwritten stories for you. Your task now is to discover these and write your own story, in which you are the hero.

Go out and conquer your dreams. Use this book as your compass, and let your inner voice guide you. You have already taken the first step by reading this book to the end. Now the rest is up to you. Because ultimately, you are the architect of your own fate.

Keep going. Dream big. And always remember: The best is yet to come!

Summary

If you are reading these lines, you have completed a remarkable journey – a journey through the world of real estate on the breathtaking island of Mallorca. But as with any good journey, the end is simply a new beginning. The path to your dream property may seem complex, but with the right strategies, the right partners, and a clear understanding of the market, this path is not only achievable but also incredibly fulfilling.

Throughout this book, we have navigated the various aspects of buying property in Mallorca. We have explored the idyllic regions and their special features and uncovered which lesser-known areas offer unexpected opportunities. You have understood the importance of a qualified real estate agent and learned criteria to select the right partner. Through strategic preparation, market analysis, and efficient budgeting, you are now armed to make informed decisions.

The long-term prospects for real estate in Mallorca are promising. Whether you use your house for vacations, as a permanent residence, or as an investment property – the choice is yours. Your vision can and should go beyond the actual purchase; consider the potential for appreciation of your property and think about possible rental options.

The real estate market in Mallorca is not a chess game where you play against the market. It's more like a dance, and with this book in hand, you now know the steps. Your dream of owning property on this paradisiacal island is not only achievable but also a life-changing experience that will broaden your horizons and raise your standard of living.
It is now up to you to take the next steps. Use this book as your reference, your source of inspiration, and your confidence booster. Let the insights of this book resonate in your decisions and actions, and step into the next phase of your adventure with confidence and enthusiasm.

It's your time. It's your journey. And your dream of Mallorca awaits to be realized. Make it happen.

Next Steps

You now stand at a crossroads. One of the most encouraging moments in life is when you realize that you are prepared, that you have the knowledge and the tools to realize your dreams. This book has provided you with a solid overview and valuable advice. Now it's time to act, and you can do so with unprecedented confidence!

First, you should clarify your priorities. What exactly are you looking for in a property? Which region of Mallorca attracts you? List your requirements and wishes and compare these with your budget. This will not only focus your search but also make the dialogue with your Mallorca real estate expert more efficient.

Next, look for a competent Mallorca real estate expert. Choosing the right partner can exponentially ease the entire purchasing process. Rely on recommendations, read reviews, and arrange initial consultations.

Now that you know the market and your options, you should not lose a moment. Time is often equivalent to money in the real estate world. Visit potential properties, analyze the condition and value of the property, and let your gut feeling speak.
Once you have found your dream home, do not hesitate. With your solid preparation and a well-thought-out strategy, you can approach the purchase process with full confidence. Remember, every property is not just a place to live but also an investment in your future.

You are just a few steps away from starting a new, exciting phase of life. A home in Mallorca is not just a building or a piece of land; it is a lifestyle, a freedom, and a piece of paradise that you can enjoy every day.

Go for it! Let your vision become reality and experience the incomparable feeling of owning your own piece of Mallorca. The island, the sea, the culture, and the opportunities are now within reach. Dare to take the next step because that is the only way dreams can come true.

7 Invaluable Benefits of Your FREE Strategy Consultation

1. Personal Expert Advice: Take the opportunity to benefit from personalized advice tailored to your specific needs and goals. No general tips, but precise, customized recommendations just for you.
2. Clear Roadmap: You will receive a clear action plan for your successful property purchase in Mallorca. Forget uncertainty and doubt; together we will determine the best path for your endeavor.

3. Time Savings: This intensive conversation will save you valuable time and help you avoid typical beginner's mistakes. We focus on what's essential so that you can make quick and efficient progress.

4. Insider Tips: Gain access to valuable insider information and strategies that are not publicly available. These are the secret tips that can make the difference between success and failure.

5. Network Access: As a participant in the strategy consultation, you get the opportunity to become part of an exclusive network. Here you will have access to contacts and resources that are not available to other buyers.

6. Financial Clarity: We will analyze your financial situation and develop strategies for getting the best terms for your property financing. This clarity is invaluable when it comes to making the right decisions.

7. Motivation and Confidence: The conversation will not only give you a clear direction but will also boost your confidence. You will leave the conversation motivated and ready to put your plans into action.

Don't miss out on these unbeatable benefits! Click on **https:/strategy consultation** or use that QR-Code

now and secure your FREE strategy consultation. It's your unique opportunity to lead your real estate project in Mallorca to success. Act now!

Your Exclusive Opportunity: FREE Strategy Consultation!

You've read the book, internalized the tips and tricks, and feel ready to take the next step? Fantastic! I want to offer you a unique opportunity to make your dream of owning property in Mallorca even more tangible.

Imagine having the chance to discuss all your burning questions, uncertainties, and specific challenges directly with an expert. A personal conversation where we analyze your individual situation together, develop a tailor-made strategy, and create a concrete action plan for your success.

That is exactly what I am offering you: a FREE, no-obligation strategy consultation!
Why shouldn't you miss this offer?
• Because it's the ultimate chance to advance your project with precise, personal, and practical advice.
• Because you will leave the conversation with a clear, step-by-step action plan.
• Because you get the advice of an experienced professional who has your success in mind.

How to participate:

Simply click on **https:/strategy consultation** and secure your spot. Spaces are limited and demand is high, so don't hesitate. Your future in Mallorca is waiting for you!

Make the decisive step that many never dare due to uncertainty. Click now and let's make your dream come true together!

Act now. Your future self will thank you.
[**https:/strategy consultation** – Secure Your FREE Strategy Consultation Now!]

About the author

Who is behind the valuable insights and extensive advice in this book? Volker Hunzelder is not only a property expert, but also an avid Mallorca lover. With decades of experience in the property industry and a deep passion for Spanish culture, he brings a unique perspective to the complex and often seemingly confusing terrain of buying property on the island.

Volker Hunzelder has made it his mission to help people find their dream home in Mallorca. Through tireless research, networking, and numerous viewings, he has built up knowledge that is as well-founded as it is practical. He didn't just want to keep this knowledge to himself; he had an unstoppable urge to share it with others. Hence this book - a condensed guide full of valuable tips, strategic advice, and authentic testimonials.

But what drives Volker Hunzelder? The answer is simple: you! He firmly believes that everyone has the right and the opportunity to create their own paradise. He wants to give you the tools to make informed decisions and realize your dream of a life under the Mallorca sun.

His journey is a source of inspiration. Starting out as a curious traveler, he has become a knowledgeable expert who now helps others find the same success. And if he could do it, so can you. This book is more than a guide; it's a testament to what's possible when passion meets expertise.

You are not just holding a book in your hands. You are holding a key to the realization of your dreams. And behind this key is Volker Hunzelder, who firmly believes that life is too short not to realize your full potential. He challenges you: Use this book as a springboard. Have the courage, take the next step and who knows - maybe you will be the next source of inspiration for all those who long for a piece of heaven on earth.

Acknowledgements

Dear readers,

At this point in our journey together, I feel a great need to pause and thank all those who have made this journey possible. The creation of this book was not just an act of writing, but a collaborative project supported by many.

Firstly, I would like to thank my family who have always encouraged me to pursue my passions. Their unconditional support has given me the strength I needed to complete this extensive work.

A big thank you also to all the professionals and property agents who have shared their in-depth knowledge and experience with me. Their expertise has made this book what it is: a valuable guide for anyone who wants to realize the dream of owning a property in Mallorca.

I am also grateful to the people of Mallorca themselves. Their hospitality and love for their homeland have inspired me time and time again. They are the heart and soul of this wonderful island and I hope to pass on some of their magic through this book.

And of course, I thank you, dear readers. You are the reason why this book was written. Your quest for knowledge, your desire to make your dreams come true, has fueled me. I sincerely hope that this book will help you to realize your own dream of Mallorca.

Before you put this book aside, take a moment to let all that you have learnt sink in. Feel the possibility that is now in your hands. You are only a few steps away from turning your dream into reality. Take this journey with confidence, armed with the knowledge and strategies you now possess.

Finally, I would like to thank the photographer Marco Richter, whose fantastic eye for the right perspective allows him to capture something special in his photos. He creates an atmosphere of emotional luxury that is unique. It was a special pleasure to work with a true professional.

With gratitude and the warmest encouragement,

Volker Hunzelder

This book is not just a conclusion, but the beginning of your new journey. Use it as your personal springboard to a future full of possibilities. Thank you for being a part of this journey.

Copyright © 2023

NAME Volker Hunzelder
ADDRESS Santa Ponca
Web: www.exclusiva-mallorca.com
E-mail: v.hunzelder@gmail.com
Tel: 0034 649 66 88 99

This work is protected by copyright.
All rights, including those of translation, reprinting and reproduction of the work or parts thereof, are reserved. No part of this work may be reproduced in any form (photocopy, microfilm, or any other process), including for educational purposes, or processed, copied, or distributed using electronic systems without the written permission of the publisher.

The reproduction of common names, trade names, product designations etc. in this work, even without special labelling, does not justify the assumption that such names are to be regarded as free within the meaning of trademark and brand protection legislation and may therefore be used by anyone. Despite careful proofreading, errors may creep in. The author and publisher are therefore grateful for any comments in this regard. All liability is excluded, all rights reserved.

© 2023 Volker Hunzelder
Edition 1
Author: Volker Hunzelder

Image rights & licenses
Images were acquired with corresponding licenses via:
https://www.pictrs.com/marcorichterphotography

Cover image: Marco Richter Nomad Photographer

Printed in Great Britain
by Amazon